Australian Biographical Monographs

16

Australian Biographical Monographs

Series Editor: Scott Prasser

Previous Volumes

Jack Lang	David Clune
Leonie Kramer	Damien Freeman
Margaret Guilfoyle	Anne Henderson
William McKell	David Clune
Neville Bonner	Sean Jacobs
George Reid	Luke Walker
Robert Askin	Paul Loughnan
John Grey Gorton	Paul Williams
Stanley Melbourne Bruce	David Lee
Robert Menzies	Scott Prasser
Neville Wran	David Clune
Lindsay Thompson	William Westerman
Johannes Bjelke-Petersen	Bruce Kingston
Harold Holt	Tom Frame
Joseph Lyons	Kevin Andrews

Australian Biographical Monographs

16

John Curtin

David Lee

Connor Court Publishing

Australian Biographical Monographs 16
John Curtin by David Lee
Published in 2022 by Connor Court Publishing Pty Ltd

Copyright © David Lee 2022

All rights reserved. No part of this book may be reproduced or transmitted in any form or by any means, electronic or mechanical, including photo copying, recording or by any information storage and retrieval system, without prior permission in writing from the publisher.

Connor Court Publishing Pty Ltd
PO Box 7257
Redland Bay QLD 4165
sales@connorcourt.com
www.connorcourt.com
Phone 0497-900-685

Printed in Australia

ISBN: 9781922815095

"Be assured of the calibre of our national character. This war may see the end of much that we have painfully and slowly built in our 150 years of existence. But even though all of it go, there will still be Australians fighting on Australian soil until the turning point be reached, and we will advance over blackened ruins, through blasted and fire-swepted cities, across scorched plains, until we drive the enemy into the sea. I give you the pledge of my country. There will always be an Australian Government and there will always be an Australian people. We are too strong in our hearts; our spirit is too high; the justice of our cause throbs too deeply in our being for that high purpose to be overcome."

> Speech to the United States, 14 March 1942,
> ABC Radio Archives

Series overview

The Connor Court Publishing's *Australian Biographical Series* on past leading Australian political leaders and other important figures seeks to provide an overview for those who are unfamiliar with the subject and to highlight the person's particular importance, controversies and contributions to Australia's progress.

The monographs are scholarly rather than academic in focus placing emphasis on a clear narrative, but with careful attention to referencing to ensure views expressed are supported by appropriate sources and evidence.

The Series was initiated because of the decline in the study of Australian history at our schools and universities and the consequential lack of knowledge or even worse, distorted views of some of Australia's leading figures who deserve to be remembered, understood for both their achievements, and as each volume also highlights, their flaws.

Acclaimed by many as Australia's greatest prime minister, John Curtin was certainly one of the most significant despite his less than four years in office. He overcame alcoholism and a troubled relationship with the Scullin Labor Government to win the Labor leadership by one vote in October 1935. Rescuing the Labor Party from division and humiliating defeats in 1931 and 1934, he put it in a position to win in the years after 1937. A constructive wartime Leader of the Opposition, he engineered the creation of an Advisory War Council to help minority Coalition and Labor governments manage a divided House of Representatives. From October 1941 he steered his wartime Labor Government through perhaps the greatest strategic challenge that Australia has ever faced. In doing so, he led Labor to one of its most emphatic electoral victories in 1943 and put his party in a position to enshrine long-held aspirations such as national control of banking and provision for a welfare state. His death in July 1945 was met with a national outpouring of grief that underlined the extent to which Curtin had been recognised as a national leader above party.

David Lee is Associate Professor in History, School of Humanities and Social Sciences, University of New South Wales, Canberra. He was General Editor of the Department of Foreign Affairs and Trade's *Documents on Australian Foreign Policy* series from 1997 to 2019. His publications on political, diplomatic, economic and strategic aspects of Australian history include *Australia and the World in the Twentieth Century* (2005), *Stanley Melbourne Bruce: Australian Internationalist* (2010) and *The Second Rush: Mining and the Transformation of Australia* (2016).

His earlier publication in Connor Court's biographical series was *Stanley Melbourne Bruce: Institution Builder* (2020). It explores Bruce's role in the creation of durable political institutions. These include the system of preferential voting introduced after Bruce's by-election win in 1918 and the federal coalition, which was formed in 1923 and supported by preferential voting. Another was the Loan Council, which was designed to co-ordinate the borrowings of state and federal governments and helped future Australian governments to navigate the Great Depression of the 1930s. Long derided as an Anglophile reactionary Bruce was a creative prime minister and long-serving diplomat.

■ Scott Prasser (Series Editor)

John Curtin

On 1 October 1935, the Federal Parliamentary Labor Party met in Canberra to elect its next leader. An exhausted James Scullin, Australia's Prime Minister from 1929 to 1931, had just stepped down as leader of the Labor Party. Scullin's resignation followed catastrophic electoral defeats in 1931 and 1934 and a devastating split in the party in New South Wales. The consensus was that Scullin would be replaced, perhaps without a ballot, by his loyal but uninspiring deputy, the Queenslander Frank Forde. Labor under Forde would probably have continued as a party of opposition, incapable of winning support at the national level. But at the last minute, the Victorian-born Member for Fremantle, John Curtin, contested the ballot.

Now fifty, Curtin had been a hard drinker prone to bouts of depression. Passed over for the Labor ministry in 1929, he had disappointed Scullin and the party's grandees by criticising the Labor Government's compromise policy to recover from the Depression, the 'Premiers' Plan'. He had lost his marginal Western Australian seat in 1931 and regained it by a relatively narrow margin in September 1934. But here were three arguments in Curtin's favour: he was one of the most powerful speakers in the House of Representatives, an omnivorous reader with electoral appeal beyond the working class and a 'clean-skin' acceptable to the warring factions in the party. To the surprise of all, he won the caucus ballot by one vote in 1935 and went on to lead the Labor Party for a decade. On 1 October 1935 enough of his colleagues recognised Curtin as a healer with the resilience to overcome adversity. Curtin's victory proved to be one of the most significant dates in the history of the Labor Party. Having risen from humble origins, Curtin developed into an outstanding leader who led Labor out of the wilderness and established it as the governing party in war and reconstruction in the 1940s.[1]

Jack Curtin: Formative Years

John Curtin was born in Creswick, in the colony of Victoria, on 8 January 1885, the eldest of four siblings in a working-class family. His parents, John Curtin and Catherine Agnes, née Bourke, were both Irish-born immigrants.[2] Curtin's father, John Curtin senior, was employed as a warder at Pentridge prison and in the police force in Creswick from 1881 to 1890.[3] He then took jobs in hotels in Melbourne and elsewhere in Victoria before eventually settling in Brunswick.[4] The Curtins' lack of money affected young John's education. He started at the state school in Creswick, but his later education was patchy. On leaving school at the age of fourteen, he became a copy boy on *The Age* newspaper, then worked as a labourer at a pottery works in Brunswick. Later he was an office boy on The *Rambler*, a bohemian weekly magazine, established with the support of artist Norman Lindsay and devoted to theatre gossip, light verse and illustrated jokes. In 1903 he started work at Titan Manufacturing Company as estimates clerk earning £2 per week.[5] The young man compensated for his incomplete schooling by spending his nights at the Melbourne Public Library. His reading embraced works on politics and economics as well as novels and, particularly, poetry.[6] Throughout his life, as Toby Davidson has shown, Curtin would use poetry to "rouse, to inform, [and] to console".[7]

He met his local state Member of Parliament, the Labor Party's Frank Anstey, around 1902, beginning a life-long friendship.[8] Anstey regarded Australia as an economic colony of the financial institutions of the City of London, described as the 'money power'.[9] He was one of several older Labor figures to whom Curtin looked for advice and guidance as he made his way in the labour movement. His meeting with Anstey came just after six British colonies federated to form the Commonwealth of Australia, a process in which Victoria evolved from 'colony' into 'state'. In the period from 1901 to the Great War from 1914 to 1918, the Labor Party, firmly based in the trade union movement, was still in its infancy. Like the nation itself, the Australian Labor Party moved gradually from a state basis to a federal structure with many stumbles and disruptions.[10] John Curtin had a ringside view of the emergence of the Labor Party and later was a participant in its development.

By 1910 a two-party system emerged with Labor as one of two major political groupings.[11] The other side of politics was initially divided between free traders and protectionists. Eventually, the anti-Labor grouping in the Federal or Commonwealth Parliament constituted itself as the Liberal Party.[12] During the Great War, the Liberals joined with pro-conscriptionist Labor MPs to form the Nationalist Party. From 1923 to 1929, the Nationalists governed in coalition with the rurally based Country Party. During the Depression years of the 1930s, the non-Labor forces reconstituted themselves again as the United Australia Party (UAP), which governed sometimes in coalition with the Country Party and at other times without it. It was not until 1944, near the end of Curtin's life that a new party, the Liberal Party, took the place of the UAP.

At the age of twenty, Curtin became Anstey's campaign manager.[13] Anstey and his friend, Frank Hyett, introduced Curtin to their Sunday morning study circle.[14] Attracted to Labor politics and socialist ideas, the young man lost his Catholic faith and gained something of a reputation as a 'Labor boy-orator' on the Yarra Bank.[15] Curtin recalled meetings each Sunday afternoon with a roster of six to eight speakers of all ages and sexes and as many as fifteen street corner meetings on Saturday nights.[16] Hyett also introduced Curtin to Tom Mann, a pioneering figure in the early labour movement in Britain, now living in Australia. Mann had emigrated to Australia because he was keen to see whether Australia's democratic franchise would be more favourable than Britain's to introduction of socialism and modification of capitalism.[17] Through Mann, who became another mentor to the young man, Curtin was introduced to a circle that included the future Victorian Premier, John Cain senior, and future Labor minister, Edward James 'Jack' Holloway.[18]

In March 1906, impatient with parliamentary

labourism, Mann founded and became Secretary of the Victorian Socialist Party (VSP).[19] The VSP quickly grew to a membership of 1,500 and produced its own weekly, *The Socialist*, which published Curtin's early writings. Among these were ideas on industrial organisation and his 1909 argument that "Australian defence policy was part and parcel of the international war policy played by the international gang of capitalists".[20] Curtin served as Honorary Secretary of the VSP in 1909 and 1910. Through it he was introduced to ideas of such British visitors as Keir Hardie, Ben Tillett and future British prime minister, Ramsay MacDonald.[21] Curtin's period in the VSP also saw him assimilate Australian poets, such as Adam Lindsay Gordon, Francis Adams and Henry Lawson with a wider reading list including works by Dante, Shakespeare, Milton, Shelley, Wordsworth and Coleridge.[22]

Curtin's connection with the labour movement as an official began in 1911 when he became General Secretary of the Timber Workers' Union.[23] The Melbourne Trades Hall Council appointed him as a member of the original disputes committee; he was also a representative on the Grand Council of Labor in 1913.[24] In the following year, Liberal Prime Minister, Joseph Cook, was granted a double dissolution election. Before polling day, however, war broke out. Australian troops were soon on the way to Europe.

At Anstey's urging, Curtin, not yet thirty, contested the federal electorate of Balaclava (now Goldstein) for the Labor Party. Balaclava was based in the wealthy inner southern suburbs of Melbourne, including Brighton and Sandringham. His opponent was the former Victorian premier, William Watt. Curtin lost the contest but polled surprisingly well in a conservative seat, winning 12,526 votes to Watt's 17,607 votes and increasing Labor's tally in the electorate by more than two thousand votes.[25] During his election campaign he proposed reducing expenditure on military organisation, including Australia's new navy, and devoting as much money as possible to what he called "aerial experiment's".[26] Specifically, he envisaged a fleet of airships stationed in the Macdonnell Ranges in the Northern Territory.[27] In domestic affairs he advocated the conventional politics of a Victorian Laborite, including a protectionist tariff, nationalisation of monopolies, a bill to give better protection to Australian industries, a strengthened Commonwealth Bank and a Commonwealth-owned line of steamers.[28] In the year of the electoral contest Curtin became the first Federal President of the Timber Workers' Union and led the campaign for the Victorian *Workers Compensation Act*.[29]

The Australian Labor Party (ALP) won the 1914 election with large majorities in the House of Representatives and the Senate. The Queenslander Andrew Fisher became Prime Minister for the third time and William Morris 'Billy' Hughes, his Attorney-General.[30] In the early years of the war Curtin was drinking heavily.[31] Curtin's drinking was exacerbated during periods of stress and loneliness. He had to leave his union post in 1915 and spend a period drying out in a convalescent home near Geelong in July 1916.[32] While he was recovering, Anstey assured him that redemption was possible and that "John drunk was a damned nuisance, but he was even in that state a better man than thousands sober, and John sober is the Nestor of them all".[33] Curtin's frailty did not stop the Australian Trades Union Anti-Conscription Congress appointing him organiser (later Secretary) of its campaign to oppose now Prime Minister Billy Hughes's objective to bring in conscription for overseas service. The labour movement was already beginning to divide about whether Australians should be compelled to fight overseas.[34] By the time Hughes returned from London in mid-1916 determined to introduce conscription, those divisions were wide.

Curtin was a passionate advocate of the anti-conscriptionist cause that succeeded in persuading Australian voters, if only by a narrow margin, to reject conscription in the first of Hughes's two plebiscites held on 28 October 1916.[35] The victory soured for Curtin when he had to serve three days in prison for refusing to comply with what he described as an illegal Military Service Proclamation calling single men into camp. Having left Melbourne to attend a conference in Sydney, a summons was left for the unmarried Curtin at his mother's house. The magistrate refused a bid by Curtin's lawyer, Maurice Blackburn, to stay the proceedings, and on 24 November sentenced him to three months imprisonment.[36] Curtin was arrested and placed in Melbourne gaol, but he was released a few days later when the Hughes Government withdrew the prosecutions.[37]

By this time Curtin was engaged to Elsie Needham. A Tasmanian born in Ballarat in 1890, Elsie had been taken to live in South Africa as a young girl.[38] She had lived in Cape Town during the Boer War and did not return to Australia until 1908. Her father, Abraham, had edited the *Socialist* newspaper in Cape Town and Elsie grew up thoroughly imbued with her father's passion for the labour cause.[39] Curtin later recalled that when he was working for the Timber Workers' Union, "I used to save up until I had £5, bought a return ticket steerage to Hobart for £4/10/-, and set out to woo my lady love with 10/- to spend on entertainment".[40] With so little to spare for entertainment, the courting couple would often make do with having an outdoor picnic.[41]

Seeking a salary that would enable him to marry, Curtin accepted a position as editor of the Australian Workers' Union's *Westralian Worker*, helped by a recommendation from Anstey.[42] On 16 February 1917 friends arranged a farewell for Jack Curtin at the Socialist Hall in Elizabeth Street, Melbourne. Anstey attended with many others to support a toast to a man he had known since he was a youth and to wish him well for new opportunities in Western Australia.[43] Elsie soon joined him in Perth and they married at the district registrar's office, Leederville, on 21 April.[44] There were only two guests, both witnesses from the *Westralian Worker*. Nor was there a honeymoon afterwards.[45]

For the next decade Curtin lived a more settled life, although he would continue to struggle intermittently with alcohol, depression and ill health. In the view of biographer David Day, Curtin's move to the West led to his reformation and rescued him from a life of "alcoholic oblivion" in Melbourne.[46] By that time,

Anstey, one of the few politicians who opposed Australia's participation in the war, was beginning to distance himself from the Labor Party and the unions to identify with what he saw as an insurgent working class. Had he stayed in Melbourne, Curtin would probably have continued to be fully imbued with Anstey's perspective; his move to the West broadened his horizons by introducing him to a more pragmatic variety of socialism. He came to Perth with a reputation as an agitator and orator, but Victor Courtney, then a *Sunday Times* editor, was surprised to meet "a slightly built, earnest looking young man ... dressed neatly and quietly" who seemed "more like a uni. professor than a leftist politician".[47]

Curtin arrived when the stocks of the local Labor Party were at a low ebb because of the split over conscription.[48] The 'Yes' majority in the Anglophile West had been large despite the defeat of conscription nationally. In the federal election held on 5 May 1917 the rump of the Labor Party led by Frank Tudor was decisively defeated. Hughes was by that time the leader of a new political organisation: the Nationalist Party. It consisted of members of the Liberal Party and pro-conscriptionist former Labor MPs such as Hughes and the Western Australian Senator and Minister for Defence, George Pearce.[49] Labor lost every Western Australian seat in the Commonwealth Parliament and won only fifteen out of fifty seats at a state election held in September 1917. The esteem in which Curtin was held led to his reluctant agreement to run as Labor candidate for the seat of Perth in the next federal election in 1919. Hughes' Nationalists won the general election convincingly and Curtin was badly beaten in Perth. Suffering from neurasthenia and melancholy, he was forced into a period of complete rest.[50] Exacerbating his depression were the deaths of his father and his close friend Hyett—the latter from Spanish influenza— in that same year.[51]

In the 1920s Curtin worked closely with another mentor, Alexander (Alick) McCallum, the General Secretary of the Western Australian Labor Party since 1914 and a fellow anti-conscriptionist.[52] McCallum found Curtin a willing ally in his campaign to rebuild the local party, a campaign for which the *Westralian Worker* was vital. The policy of the paper was to support any campaign for the improvement of labour, politically or industrially. With Curtin's help, McCallum won the South Fremantle seat in the Legislative Assembly in 1921 and became one of the lieutenants of Philip Collier, who led his party to a narrow victory and became Premier after the elections of 1924.

Twelve years older than Curtin, Collier was also born in Melbourne and had served as campaign director for state and federal Labor candidates, including Anstey, in the late 1890s and early 1900s.[53] He had moved to Western Australia in 1904 and shortly afterwards was elected to the eastern goldfields seat of Boulder in the Legislative Assembly. In 1911 Collier became a minister in the Labor administration of John Scaddan and adopted a forthright stance against conscription during the Great War. Indeed, in March 1918, Collier was fined by a magistrate for utterances during the second conscription plebiscite "likely to cause disaffection".⁵⁴ Curtin, too, was fined £15 in 1917 for similar anti-conscriptionist utterances.⁵⁵ Collier and McCallum became two of the strongest supporters of the new editor of the *Westralian Worker*.

Over ten years and hundreds of articles and editorials, Curtin made the weekly *Westralian Worker* probably the best Labor paper in Australia.⁵⁶ He was Western Australian District President of the Australian Journalists' Association from 1920 to 1925 and a friend of the foundation professors of English and History at the University of Western Australia, Walter Murdoch and Edward Shann, both originally Victorians.⁵⁷ In 1923 John and Elsie Curtin, now proud parents of son John and daughter Elsie, moved into a modest red-brick bungalow in Cottesloe. Curtin gained a large measure of stability from family life and enjoyed spending time with his young children. At this time Curtin was a socialist in the Anstey mould, but his experience in Western Australia and the influence of politicians such as McCallum and Collier brought about a gradual change.

In Perth he gradually reached the view that the only realistic way of achieving meaningful social and political change was through the agency of parliamentary action by the Labor Party, which held office in Western Australia from 1911 to 1914 and from 1924 to 1930. Curtin became doubtful, too, of the advantages that some radical socialists and Australian Communists saw in promoting strike action. This led to a falling out between Curtin and the Australian Seamen's Union led by Tom Walsh, an Irish-born Australian Communist.⁵⁸

Walsh had married the suffragette, Adela Pankhurst, who had appeared with Curtin in addressing socialist gatherings in Melbourne.[59] Under Walsh's leadership, incessant strike action (called 'job control') had led to the Arbitration Court's deregistration of the Seamen's Union in 1925. Following the subsequent strike by the Seamen's Union, members of the union passed a resolution calling Curtin 'black', meaning that they would allow no ship to carry him as a passenger.[60] While the resolution was eventually rescinded, the incident illustrated the degree to which Curtin had distanced himself from both his earlier revolutionary socialism, and from strike action taken outside Commonwealth or state arbitration systems.

In mid-1924 the Commonwealth Government, now a coalition between the Nationalists, led by Stanley Melbourne Bruce, and the Country Party, headed by Dr Earle Page, asked the state governments to nominate a delegate to represent Australia at the International Labour Organisation in Geneva.[61] Curtin initially declined the nomination on learning that he would not be compensated for loss of salary while away from Australia. When the Bruce Government agreed to support part of his lost salary, he accepted. Curtin attended the conference and returned to Australia with a better appreciation of the League of Nations and the International Labour Organisation (ILO). He also used his overseas trip profitably to go to England to meet various socialists. After his return, he was critical of the lack of Commonwealth support for the ILO, particularly its dilatoriness in ratifying its conventions. He was disapproving, too, of the lack of participation in the conference by the Commonwealth's chief delegate, the High Commissioner in the United Kingdom, Sir Joseph Cook, and the burden this placed on the two delegates nominated by labour and the employers and Osmond Fuhrman, an official at Australia House, London.[62]

In the following year, after the national seamen's strike, Curtin stood as the Labor candidate for the federal seat of Fremantle.[63] In 1925 he was forty years of age and described as one of best candidates on either side of politics.[64] His opponent was William Watson, a Fremantle-based businessman, two of whose sons had been killed in the First World War.[65] Watson had won the seat of Fremantle as an independent in 1922. An outspoken critic of the party system, he usually voted with the government parties in the House of Representatives. At the 1925 election, which focused heavily on the Communist menace to Australia, Watson convincingly won the ballot with 20,568 votes to Curtin's 14,812 votes.[66]

When Curtin contested the election again in 1928, Watson had retired as Member for Fremantle. The Nationalists endorsed as their candidate Frank Gibson, a pharmacist and member for the state seat of Fremantle from 1921 to 1924. Gibson had lived in Western Australia since 1902. For some years he was on the goldfields and had been Mayor of Leonora from 1912 to 1914.[67] The 1928 contest was complicated when an accountant, Keith Watson, entered the ring.[68] Watson identified himself as a Nationalist although he was not endorsed by that party. His entry into the contest increased Curtin's chances by raising the prospect of splitting the non-Labor vote. Even so, the *West Australian* newspaper predicted that, since Curtin had lost by a margin of more than 6,000 votes in 1925, he was unlikely to overcome that deficit in 1928.[69]

By 1928, however, Curtin's political standing in Western Australia had been elevated by service in 1927 and 1928 on the Commonwealth Royal Commission on Child Endowment or Family Allowances.[70] Curtin was irritated by the majority view that the cost of child endowment would be too expensive for the Commonwealth to bear and, with Mildred Muscio, produced a powerful minority report. Muscio, a school principal based in Sydney, was a zealous advocate for the rights of women and children and President of the National Council of Women from 1927 to 1929.[71]

By 1928 there were already some signs of an economic downturn in Australia that was affecting the popularity of the Bruce–Page Government. Labor's stocks at the federal level rose when, on 29 March 1928, James Scullin, one of parliament's best orators, succeeded Matthew Charlton as Leader of the Opposition.[72] Scullin and Curtin had forged an alliance during Curtin's involvement in Labor and trade union politics in Melbourne before 1917.[73] In the contest for Fremantle in November 1928, Curtin charged the Bruce Government with increasing Australian taxes, boosting overseas debt, and converting a huge budget surplus into a deficit. In opening the campaign in the Fremantle Town Hall, he spoke for an hour and a half to wide acclaim. One young woman in the audience observed: "You could hear a pin drop when he was speaking ... people admired him because every word he said they knew he believed in, and what he said was the truth".[74]

Curtin went into the contest with the backing of Collier, who described him "as among the ablest men in public life" and added that his "election to the Commonwealth Parliament would give Western Australia a splendid advocate".[75] Curtin was assisted by the turning of the tide against the Bruce Government throughout Australia, although it retained office. Curtin won Fremantle in 1928 at the same time as Ben Chifley, Curtin's successor as prime minister, secured the New South Wales seat of Macquarie for Labor.[76] Curtin entered the House of Representatives at the age of 43 with a decade behind him as editor of one of Labor's best national newspapers and years of experience as a grassroots campaigner for the labour movement. He was an avid reader of works on economics and political economy such as by John Maynard Keynes and Arthur Pigou. This was attested by those who saw his library in Cottesloe: a large and eclectic collection including the novels of Edgar Wallace and works of poetry, textbooks on philosophy, and works on history, finance and international affairs.[77] When Curtin made the long rail journey from Fremantle to Canberra, Anstey, who had represented the northern Melbourne seat of Bourke since 1910, was delighted to welcome his friend into the caucus. In February 1929 his colleagues showed their esteem for Curtin by electing him to the caucus executive.[78] Curtin faced a particular challenge as a Member of Parliament

(MP) from Western Australia. This meant having to make frequent and arduous trips back and forth over the nearly four thousand kilometres that separated Fremantle from Canberra, the nation's capital.

In 1929, despite its victory in the 1928 election, Bruce faced increasing political pressure. In August Scullin moved a no confidence motion against his government. This was in response to Bruce's decision earlier in the year to drop a prosecution of colliery owner John Brown for his role in locking out mineworkers in the Hunter Valley.[79] The motion was defeated but Billy Hughes and Edward Mann, the Nationalist Member for Perth, voted with the Labor Opposition. Bruce then introduced the Maritime Industries Bill which sought to abolish the Commonwealth Court of Conciliation and Arbitration and hand back most of the Commonwealth's powers over industrial relations to the states.

Curtin was highly critical of the initiative and sought to refute charges made by Nationalist Senator George Pearce that increasing industrial lawlessness justified the move.[80] Curtin pointed out that the great majority of Australia's industrial disputes originated in New South Wales. Except for the coal mining industry and shipping services, Curtin argued, industrial disputes in Australia were less frequent and smaller, in relation to population, than those in Britain or the United States. Strikes against the arbitration system, leaving aside coal miners and timber workers who were both involved in bitter disputes at the time, were rare.[81]

At the committee stage of the bill, a proposal was made that the legislation should not be implemented until

Bruce had either faced an election or put the question for approval to the people in a referendum. Bruce treated this as a vote of no confidence in the government and advised the Governor-General to call an election for the House of Representatives alone on 12 October 1929.[82] On this occasion, Curtin contested Fremantle against Keith Watson as the endorsed Nationalist candidate. Watson was happy to campaign on a platform of states' rights and against the centralisation of power in the Commonwealth government.[83] He also made some play with the apparent inconsistency of his opponent. Curtin had opposed Bruce's referendum in 1926 seeking to centralise powers over industrial relations in the Commonwealth and then resisted the 1929 effort to hand back industrial powers to the states.[84] Curtin did not favour either complete centralisation of Commonwealth power favoured by some of his federal Labor colleagues or the states' rights conception of Watson; he stood for a balance of responsibilities between Commonwealth and states.

Curtin decisively defeated his Nationalist opponent with 24,482 votes against Watson's 18,426.[85] The election itself was an emphatic victory for Labor, thus ending thirteen years in opposition with what was then its largest ever majority in the House of Representatives. In all, Labor won 46 seats to the Coalition's 24. Adding to the disaster for the Coalition was that five ministers lost their seats, including Bruce himself, who was defeated in Flinders by Curtin's friend, Holloway.[86]

The Scullin Government and the Great Depression, 1929–34

Despite Curtin's comparatively short time in the Commonwealth Parliament, keen observers predicted that he was likely to earn a place in the new Labor cabinet. After the caucus vote, Scullin became Prime Minister, former Queensland Premier Edward Theodore, Treasurer, and Joseph Lyons, a Catholic former schoolteacher, and former Premier of Tasmania, the Postmaster-General.[87] Anstey was appointed Minister for Health and Frank Brennan Attorney-General. Holloway was rewarded with the position of Assistant Minister to the Treasurer while Jack Beasley, Member for West Sydney and still in his thirties, entered the ministry as Minister assisting the Minister for Industry. Curtin, albeit narrowly, missed out on election to the ministry.[88] Part of the reason was that his close relationship with Anstey was held against him by Theodore; both Scullin and Theodore worried about his drinking; and the deeply religious Scullin was disappointed that Curtin had renounced his church.[89]

The first months of the Scullin Government brought more disappointments for Curtin as the euphoria that accompanied Labor's victory in 1929 evaporated. The Scullin Government faced rapidly rising unemployment, increasing industrial turbulence, economic depression and financial crisis. It also encountered repeated obstruction from the Commonwealth Bank Board and a Senate dominated by the Opposition and determined to block unorthodox economic policies. When the

Scullin Government took office, the international debt of the Commonwealth and the states stood at £631 million, and most of this sum was owed to bondholders in Great Britain. British financiers, Anstey's 'Kingdom of Shylock', compounded difficulties by deciding not to lend any more money to Australia.[90] This problem was exacerbated because prices of wool and wheat plummeted in 1929–30.[91]

On 21 November 1929, Scullin raised the tariff on three hundred items and added an emergency 'primage' duty. The best indicator of the general level of protection, the British Preferential Tariff, nearly doubled between 1928–29 and 1931–32. Curtin supported measures to strengthen protection for Australian industry. These measures were necessary, he argued, "to correct Australia's trade balance, to assist our industries and place Australia in a position to meet its international obligations".[92] Imports dropped obligingly from £143 million in 1928–29 to a mere £44 million three years later. Australia could not, however, sell more exports abroad. As the prices of staple commodities fell and income from abroad diminished, the Scullin Government found it increasingly difficult to meet the interest payment on overseas debt.

During Scullin's short-lived government, Australia teetered on the edge of insolvency as it struggled to pay its financial obligations to British lenders. In January 1930 Australia had effectively left the 'gold standard'— the international financial system by which currencies were convertible into gold on demand and linked by fixed rate of exchange—by prohibiting export of gold.

Besides taking Australia off the gold standard, the Scullin Government took what practical measures it could, including cutting spending on defence and immigration.[93] It also sought to encourage exports by guaranteeing a minimum price to Australian wheat growers. But although Australian wheat production increased, a glut on global markets further reduced wheat prices. The Scullin Government was unable to pay the promised minimum price and many farmers were ruined. Curtin, not a member of the ministry, was freed to go back to Western Australia at the request of his caucus colleagues. They asked him to support Collier in an election on 12 April 1930.[94] But despite Curtin's support, Collier's Labor Party was defeated by a Nationalist – Country Party coalition led by James Mitchell.

In June 1930 Scullin announced that Sir Otto Niemeyer from the Bank of England would be visiting Australia to advise the government about its economic predicament.[95] The visit reflected growing concern on the part of the British Treasury and the Bank of England that Australian policies such as protectionism, wage arbitration and excessive borrowing had put Australia on an unsustainable economic path. Niemeyer advised all the governments, federal and state, that Australia's standard of living was too high and that the governments had to balance their budgets. In deference to Niemeyer's advice, the governments, in what was known as the 'Melbourne Agreement', committed themselves to strong spending cuts. Curtin was strongly critical of Niemeyer's prescriptions and the Melbourne Agreement. The latter was eventually killed off by election of the Labor Government under Jack Lang in New South Wales in October 1930. As Premier of Australia's most populous state, Lang was emphatic that he would have no truck with either Niemeyer or British bondholders.

Curtin opposed the Scullin Government's policy of deflation. He urged ministers to resist cuts to wages and pensions of Australians and to pursue measures that reflated the economy. One such inflationary measure was devaluation of the Australian pound. In January 1931, it was in fact devalued as a means of stemming the inflow of imports and boosting exports. Other inflationary proposals were Theodore's advocacy of a program of public works and expansion of credit through issue of 'fiduciary notes', banknotes printed by the government without the backing of gold.[96]

Curtin strongly and publicly supported Theodore's measures, including his plan to create a Central Reserve Bank. For Curtin such a bank would serve two great purposes. It would help Australians to pool their financial resources and give the Commonwealth Parliament a direct "responsibility for the credit policy of Australia".[97] Curtin, however, was no mere passive supporter of the ministry. He challenged the view of both Scullin and Theodore on occasions. One was over their initial unwillingness to assist the gold industry, which was of considerable importance to his state. With the support of the Western Australian financier, Claude de Bernales, Curtin eventually persuaded the Scullin Government to introduce a bonus as an incentive to produce gold.[98] He saw this as a means of stimulating the industry and attracting foreign investment to it.[99]

Although Scullin and the Labor caucus backed the Theodore plan, it was rejected by the Senate. The Commonwealth Bank, dominated by a board of businessmen and led by its conservative chairman, Sir Robert Gibson, would not co-operate either.[100] The Commonwealth Bank, in thrall to the orthodox prescriptions of the Bank of England, demanded stringent expenditure cuts from the Scullin Government. Theodore's unsuccessful pursuit of his plan was delivered a further blow when he was accused of engaging in corrupt financial dealings as Premier of Queensland. In 1930 Theodore had to step aside as Treasurer while the matter was investigated.[101] He made way, temporarily, for the more conservative Joseph Lyons as Acting Treasurer. Matters worsened for Curtin when Scullin and his ministers concluded that some measure of deflation could not be avoided. In January 1931 the Commonwealth Arbitration Court cut the basic wage by ten per cent. The result of this measure, as historian Frank Bongiorno has set out, was that real wages in Australia fell to about the same level as in the United States, which had a much freer labour market than Australia. They also fell more sharply than in Britain, which did not have a centralised wage fixing system but had relatively strong trade unions.[102]

Throughout the latter stages of 1930 Curtin became increasingly frustrated by the Scullin Government's inability to implement its main political agenda. This frustration was somewhat alleviated in January 1931 when Scullin reappointed Theodore as Treasurer. By this time, Scullin and Theodore were being assailed from the left as well as the right. Jack Lang had introduced his own plan to combat the Depression.[103] At the core of the so-called Lang Plan was that Australia should suspend payment of interest to British bondholders and divert the funds saved to measures of unemployment relief. At that time, state governments, rather than the Commonwealth Government, provided the meagre unemployment relief that was available to the swelling numbers of unemployed Australians. To conservative critics and the Scullin Labor Government, Lang's prescriptions amounted to repudiation of Australia's overseas debts.

On the backbench, depressed about the policies of the Scullin Government and lonely, Curtin took to drinking.[104] Writing to Elsie, he complained that life was "rotten" in Canberra, not to mention "cold as the North Pole".[105] The sense that Curtin's talents were not appreciated was underlined on 13 November 1930 when the *Sydney Morning Herald*'s Canberra correspondent wrote:

> Oratorically, he is the richest asset of the Labor Party, and it would not be extravagant to say that he is by far the finest rhetorician in the House. Moreover, it is on the subject of finance that he expresses himself best, although his views are unorthodox.[106]

Part of Curtin's appeal as an orator, Davidson has argued, was "his unabashed idealism, his sense of shared purpose".[107] This idealism was mixed with a melancholy that was exacerbated when he missed out on another opportunity to join the ministry in 1931. Disgusted by Theodore's return to the Treasury, Lyons resigned from the ministry in January and from the Labor Party in mid-March. Accompanied by another senior member of the Scullin Government, James Fenton, and four other conservative Labor members, Lyons then crossed the floor to sit on the Opposition benches. The resignations of Lyons and Fenton created an opportunity for Curtin to enter the ministry. But when he learned that Anstey had been 'dumped', Curtin quietly let his colleagues know not to vote for him.[108] Ben Chifley was a beneficiary, elected by caucus and appointed Minister for Defence on 3 March 1931.

In mid-1931 the Scullin Government reached an agreement with the state premiers on another scheme, known as the Premiers' Plan, that appeared to Curtin to be a complete abrogation of Labor principles. The plan contained a mixture of deflationary and inflationary elements with the former dominating. It envisaged three years of cuts in government expenditure as well as increases in taxation. To that extent the plan was deflationary, but there were inflationary elements as well. One was that, as government deficits would be financed by selling treasury bills to private banks, the effect would be to increase the size of the money supply. Another was that the plan envisaged reducing the rate of interest on Australian loans owed to local bondholders. But for Curtin, the Premiers' Plan would not be implemented by governments in consultation with their parliaments but rather with an "outside junta of bankers".[109] He told an audience in Perth in

June 1931 that the Scullin Government should force a double dissolution on its financial policy and go to the people or resign.[110]

> The programme of the [Premiers'] Conference was the programme of the Nationalist Party, the leader of which should put it into operation. If the Premiers' Plan meant that there was to be a paramount regard for money and less regard for human welfare, no Labor Government worthy of the name should make the sacrifice.[111]

In July 1931 Curtin voiced his criticisms openly in the House of Representatives when he attacked the Premiers' Plan as involving reversal of the earlier position of the Scullin Government, namely, to rehabilitate industry, in favour of a policy of simply balancing budgets.[112] To his mind it was extraordinary that Scullin and Theodore could expect prices to recover in Australia while salaries of wage earners and pensions were lowered. Theodore was clearly stung by the speech, chiding Curtin—in pointedly personal terms given his alcoholism— as "drunk with his own rhetoric".[113]

By this time, conservative businessmen and anti-Labor figures had been impressed by Lyons' performance as Acting Treasurer They approved his obeisance to the principles of 'sound finance' and his stance against unorthodox ideas of Labor politicians such as Theodore and Curtin.[114] By May 1931 they had succeeded in establishing a new political party to succeed the old Nationalist Party that had been established by Hughes in 1917. The new political party, the United Australia

Party (UAP), was led by Lyons with the former leader of the Nationalist Party, John Latham, as his deputy. The defection of Lyons and some of his allies from the Labor Party weakened the Scullin Government, but it was kept in power in the second half of 1931 by the adherents of Jack Lang in the Commonwealth Parliament. Towards the end of the year, however, they crossed the floor over what seemed a minor matter and brought an end to the Scullin Government.[115] 'Stabber Jack' Beasley, later a minister under Curtin, became the leader of the 'Langite' rebels in the House of Representatives.

In the ensuing general election on 19 December, Labor suffered a humiliating defeat and was left with only 18 seats between the 14 official Australian Labor Party representatives (Scullin Labor) and the four adherents of Lang.[116] The 'Langites' did not caucus with official Labor until 1936. The United Australia Party, with 34 seats, gained the support of five South Australian members from the Emergency Committee of South Australia, which had contested the election in that state. This meant that the UAP could govern by itself and did not need to form a coalition with the Country Party, still led by Earle Page. Curtin was not exempt from the national backlash against Labor. William Watson entered the ring once more to contest the seat against Curtin and the endorsed UAP candidate, Keith Watson. Curtin received 19,142 votes, William Watson 14,092 and Keith Watson 12,365. When Keith Watson was eliminated from the count, his preferences gave William Watson a comfortable majority and Curtin was now out of the House of Representatives.[117]

The electoral defeat was a mixed blessing for Curtin as he was forced to leave behind a period of severe stress and heavy drinking in Canberra for three years of a more settled family life in Fremantle.[118] There he freelanced for daily and interstate newspapers and corresponded intermittently with Theodore with whom he had something of a reconciliation.[119] In mid-1932, the Perth Trades Hall appointed him a publicity officer and he also contributed a column to the *Westralian Worker* on racing, although he hardly ever gambled himself.[120]

In the following year, the people of Western Australia voted in a plebiscite to secede from the Commonwealth of Australia while also returning a Collier-led Labor Government that was opposed to secession. Collier appointed Curtin full-time chairman, on a salary of £12 per week, of a committee to prepare the Western Australian case before the new Commonwealth Grants Commission, which had been set up in 1933 to help the smaller states in the Federation and make them more amenable to staying in the Commonwealth.[121] Curtin worked for about a year in preparing the case. While Curtin was totally opposed to secession, he also disagreed with some in his party who proposed unification, that is abolition of the states. Unlike many of his colleagues, Curtin had reached the view that, while the Constitution should be reformed, there should be a balance of responsibilities between Commonwealth and states. Curtin's moderation on both unification (abolishing the states) and the party's 1921 "socialist objective" was part of the reason for his electoral appeal in later campaigns in 1940 and 1943.

Leader of the Opposition, 1935-39

By 1934, the year the next federal election was due, the defeated Member for Fremantle and his friends were hopeful of his being able to return to the Commonwealth Parliament. Already some were talking about Curtin as a potential successor to the exhausted Scullin as leader of the Labor Party.[122] Early in 1934 Curtin toyed with the idea of standing for Bourke, Anstey's electorate in northern Melbourne.[123] This was a logical move given that Bourke included Brunswick, where Curtin had once lived and worked, and where his mother and relatives still resided. Eventually, he decided to remain in Western Australia and to stand once again for Fremantle from which William Watson had announced his retirement for a second time. Curtin campaigned on the need to develop national policies to combat the Great Depression.[124]

In Curtin's mind the states had been forced to bear the brunt of the costs of high unemployment, while the Commonwealth, notwithstanding its higher taxing capacity, had done comparatively little. He also pointed out that Western Australia and Queensland, both with Labor governments, had performed better than other states in having the lowest percentage of unemployed. Curtin argued that the Commonwealth should use its taxing powers to help balance the budgets of the states, that the Commonwealth Bank should be empowered to compete with the trading banks, and that the value of wages, pensions and social services should be restored.[125]

With William Watson no longer in the contest for

Fremantle, Curtin had to consider who would be his main opponent. Keith Watson, seen as a likely candidate, had been chosen as one of the Western Australian delegates to argue the case for secession before the Westminster Parliament.[126] Eventually the UAP settled on Florence Cardell-Oliver, President of the Perth Branch of the Women's Service Guild and an author of a book variously titled *On Empire Unity* or *Red Asiatic Domination*. The *Westralian Worker* portrayed her as having "slipped badly both over the air and at public meetings" in her campaign.[127] It also mocked the major theme of her campaign, that of persistently seeking to link Communism and Moscow with the Australian Labor Party and its candidate.[128] Curtin's friends, however, were too optimistic about an easy win for Labor over the UAP candidate. Cardell-Oliver put up a strong fight, polling surprisingly well in subdivisions regarded as Labor strongholds and gaining a big advantage in affluent Claremont, the largest subdivision in the electorate.[129]

In the end, after counting of postal and absent votes and allocation of Social Credit preferences, Curtin eked out a narrow victory of 24,951 votes to Cardell-Oliver's 23,923.[130] Having won Fremantle, a marginal seat, Curtin resolved that he would not switch seats and that his ultimate political fate would be determined by the voters of Fremantle.[131] In this sense, he distinguished himself from Billy Hughes who had switched from Bendigo, the seat to which he moved after leaving Labor in 1916, to the safer seat of North Sydney in 1922. Unlike Curtin, Hughes was as promiscuous with his electorates as with his parties.

There was an element of risk, however, in Curtin's decision to stay in Fremantle, as would be made all too clear in 1940.

Although the Labor Party's share of the primary vote fell to an even lower proportion in 1934 than in 1931, it nevertheless won four seats on preferences including Curtin's seat of Fremantle.[132] At the same time, the New South Wales Labor Party, whose members were loyal to Jack Lang, increased its membership by an extra five seats to nine in total. In poor health, Scullin resigned as Leader of the Opposition on 1 October 1935. Scullin's deputy, the Queenslander Frank Forde, had all the 'big battalions' on his side and Scullin's support to succeed him.[133] Some thought that the ballot would go uncontested, but Holloway, the old Victorian anti-conscriptionist union official encouraged Curtin to stand if he pledged not to drink alcohol.[134] Curtin agreed to give up drinking alcohol altogether.[135] Thereafter, in place of whisky, Curtin turned to cigarettes, smoking forty a day.[136] To the surprise of all, Curtin made up for his narrow loss in the 1929 ballot for the Scullin ministry. He won the ballot for leader of the party by one vote, eleven to ten.[137] Ironically, a crucial vote for Curtin was that of Maurice Blackburn, who had defended Curtin against prosecution in 1916 and succeeded Anstey in the seat of Bourke. Blackburn, who by now reciprocated Curtin's personal dislike for him, only relented at the last moment by allowing another MP to cast a proxy vote for the Member for Fremantle.[138] When Scullin, who had voted for Forde, heard of the result, he exclaimed, "It can't be right".[139]

Curtin's election to the Labor leadership was surprising for two reasons. He had been an opponent of the Premiers' Plan, and no major party leader had ever come from Western Australia; ironically, in 1913 Joseph Cook had won the leadership of the Liberal Party by one vote, defeating the legendary Western Australian, Sir John Forrest. On the other hand, being out of Parliament between 1931 and 1934 gave Curtin an advantage in not being too closely identified with either of the warring factions in the Labor Party: the Federal Labor Party loyal to Scullin and the New South Wales Labor Party which was predominantly loyal to Jack Lang. As an opponent of the Premiers' Plan, Curtin was the man most likely to effect a reconciliation with Lang.[140]

Lang's adherents in the Commonwealth Parliament had brought down the Scullin Government for executing the Premiers' Plan. Lang as Premier of New South Wales sought to persist with his plan to cease interest payments to bondholders in Great Britain. To protect Australia's international credit, Prime Minister Joseph Lyons had the Commonwealth pay interest payments of New South Wales and sought to recoup the money from the New South Wales Treasury by passing the *Financial Agreement Enforcement Act* 1932. Lang protested that the actions of the Commonwealth prevented New South Wales from paying the salaries of state employees and, rather implausibly, that this constituted an act of slavery, which had been illegal in the British Empire since 1834. Lang then withdrew the funds from the New South Wales Treasury to stop Commonwealth authorities from getting access to the money. At this point the Governor of New South Wales, Sir Philip Game, withdrew Lang's commission as Premier and appointed the UAP leader, Bertram Stevens. Stevens immediately called an election at which the Labor Party was heavily defeated.[141] Lang continued to lead the Opposition in the New South Wales Parliament until 1939 and fought two further elections, in 1935 and 1938, in both of which he was defeated.[142]

Curtin appreciated that if the Labor Party were to be successful in winning office again at the national level, then the federal party had to be united. To that end he toured state executives and local centres. In October 1935 he persuaded the Federal Executive of the Labor Party to call a unity conference with the New South Wales Labor Party.[143] The result of this initiative was that by February 1936 Jack Beasley, Eddie Ward and other 'Langites' had joined the Labor caucus.[144]

In the second half of the 1930s Curtin had to navigate some tricky foreign policy issues that had the potential to split the Labor Party. One was Italy's invasion of the independent African country, Abyssinia (Ethiopia), in 1935. The aim of Italy's Fascist Government, led by Benito Mussolini, was to incorporate the African kingdom into the Italian empire by force.[145] In Great Britain the Government and the Labour Opposition supported the League of Nations in imposing economic sanctions on Italy for what they saw as an act of blatant aggression. The Lyons Government initially followed the lead of the British Government, but some of its key members and the High Commissioner, in London,

Stanley Melbourne Bruce, were doubtful of the efficacy of sanctions. Curtin struggled to find a compromise that could unite those party members who were supportive of the League of Nations and others who adopted an isolationist stance.[146] Curtin ultimately came out against sanctions against Italy. In 1936, Italy made a new advance using poison gas and entered the Ethiopian capital, Addis Ababa, on 5 May. Maurice Blackburn, whose vote had helped Curtin defeat Forde in 1935, now defied Curtin by voting for sanctions against Italy. The Labor Party expelled him for his support for the Victorian Council of the Movement against War and Fascism in December 1935; he was not reinstated until Easter 1937.[147]

It was on defence policy, however, that Curtin was able clearly to differentiate Labor policy from that of the Lyons Government, which following the 1934 elections had become a coalition between the UAP and the Country Party. By the mid-1930s, the Australian and British governments had developed the Singapore naval defence strategy as their main means of countering possible Japanese aggression in the Asia-Pacific. Formulated between 1919 and 1941, the plan aimed to deter aggression by Japan, the strongest naval power in Asia, by providing a base for the Royal Navy in the Far East. From such a base, it was hoped, elements of the Royal Navy would be able to intercept and defeat a Japanese force heading south against India or Australia.[148] In 1919, the British Government chose Singapore, at the eastern end of the Strait of Malacca, as the site of the base. Work to develop the base, while interrupted by financial stringencies, extended over the next two decades. British defence planners envisaged that, in a war with Japan, the garrison would defend the fortified naval base until the Royal Navy could steam from the Atlantic Ocean to Singapore. The Royal Navy would then relieve or recapture the British Crown Colony of Hong Kong and blockade the Japanese Islands to force the Japanese to negotiate.

During the early 1920s, when Curtin was still editing the *Westralian Worker*, the Labor Opposition in the Federal Parliament, had sketched an alternative to the Singapore strategy: a powerful air force as a first line of defence supported by a well-equipped army capable of rapid expansion to meet any threat of invasion. Curtin had foreshadowed aspects of this policy in his 1914 campaign for Balaclava. Some officers in the Australian Army made similar criticisms of the Singapore strategy in the late 1920s and 1930s. In 1927 Lieutenant-Colonel Henry Wynter published an article in the British *Army Quarterly* casting doubt on whether Britain, if it were also involved in a war in Europe, would be able to send sufficient naval resources to Singapore.[149] Advocates of the Singapore strategy included Curtin's future chief defence adviser, Frederick Shedden. They countered that a naval strategy was essential because Australia would still be vulnerable to a naval blockade even if it were able to resist an actual invasion.

In 1936 Curtin used a further statement by Wynter of these arguments to cast doubt on the viability of the Singapore strategy.[150] "How", Curtin asked, "could the British Fleet send sufficient ships to the western Pacific to prevent offensive operations there by an eastern first-class power, if Britain was engaged in a European war"?[151] Curtin's thinking was that Australia could not, from its own resources, afford a navy equal to that of a world power. But it should, and could, afford to "maintain an Air Force equal to any which could be brought against her".[152] Harking back to his 1914 campaign for Balaclava, Curtin called for the strengthening of Australia's land and air forces and larger oil supplies to allow greater self-reliance in defence policy.

Curtin approached the 1937 election in an ebullient mood, anticipating that the Labor Party would be able to pick up enough seats in the House of Representatives to form a government.[153] One of the reasons for the change of mood was that Labor won the seat of Gwydir at a by-election in May. This seemed to indicate that Curtin had finally turned the "tide of voters' disapproval of the Federal ALP".[154] Broadcasting Labor's election policy speech from Perth, on 20 September 1937, he made a robust defence of Labor's contribution to Australia's recovery from the Great Depression.[155] By his estimation, Scullin's conversion of loans to lower interest rates under its *Financial Emergency Act* had saved Australians £46 million in interest payments. This he contrasted with the efforts of the High Commissioner in London, Stanley Melbourne Bruce, in converting overseas loans, which had saved just over £11 million.[156] Similarly, he pointed out that Scullin's re-arrangement of payments on Australia's war debt had saved Australians £32,200,000 annually. He then attacked the Lyons Government for promising action on unemployment insurance, housing and youth but then doing nothing.[157]

Curtin also built on the work of the 1935–37 Commonwealth appointed Royal Commission on Monetary and Banking Systems, of which his former caucus colleague, Ben Chifley, had been a member on Curtin's nomination.[158] Throughout his younger life, Curtin had made a habit of attaching himself to older male mentors, such as Mann, McCallum and Anstey. These relationships had not always helped Curtin. In 1929, for example, his friendship with Anstey was enough for Theodore to deny him a ministry in the Scullin Government. By middle age, however, Curtin was less apt to defer to mentors and more willing to make his own judgements. This is illustrated by Curtin's relationship with Anstey. Now retired, the latter angled to be appointed to the banking royal commission, but Curtin took the view that the long-term interests of the Labor Party were better served by appointment of Chifley. Curtin had a shrewd intuition that Chifley, out of Parliament since 1931, would get back to the House of Representatives.[159] Chifley's work on the Royal Commission provided valuable training for his later work as Treasurer in the Curtin Labor Government.

Insisting that national control of credit was essential, Curtin promised that a Labor Government would legislate for the Commonwealth Bank to control credit for the nation, rates of interest, direction of general investment and currency relations with external markets.[160] For defence, Curtin promised to increase the strength of the Air Force to an aerial fleet of 25 squadrons and 300 aircraft. In addition, Curtin promised to take "every legislative" step to establish a forty-hour week, to work towards a scheme of national insurance and unemployment relief and organised marketing of primary products.[161]

In the election on 23 October 1937 the party's only gains in the House of Representatives were two seats, Ballarat (Victoria) and Gwydir (NSW), the latter originally won by William Scully in a by-election on 8 May 1937.[162] But Labor's position had improved considerably under Curtin's leadership. Unification of Federal Labor with the New South Wales branch in 1936 meant that the ALP's total numbers stood at 29 seats, its best performance since 1929. The Coalition still had a comfortable majority, the UAP having won 28 seats and the Country Party 15 seats; but in terms of the two-party-preferred vote, Labor won almost half. Having not won any Senate seats at the 1934 election, Labor picked up 16 out of 19 seats contested; the Coalition parties with 20 seats still had a comfortable majority.[163] For one observer of politics, Don Whitington, the real significance of the 1937 election was not so much its outcome as Labor's advances in development of policy.[164] Had the Labor Party voted for Forde and not Curtin in 1935, Whitington argued, "the party would have continued to follow the vacillating, almost pusillanimous path that Labor had pursued since the Conscription disaster".[165]

In the year after the election, the British Labour parliamentarian Hugh Dalton visited Australia and provided a perceptive appreciation of the Australian

Labor leader.[166] Dalton was subsequently minister in Winston Churchill's wartime coalition Government and Chancellor of the Exchequer for a time in Clement Attlee's post-war Labour Government. While at sea Dalton received a radio message from Curtin, who met him at the ship in Fremantle on 11 January 1938 and then spent some time with him. Dalton described Curtin as:

> by general consent, the best speaker in the Federal Parliament, and I was told able to move great audiences as no other political leader in Australia. His opponents feared him on radio at the last election. He is an idealist with his feet on the ground, a thoughtful student of politics, honest and clear headed, with a dislike for the exaggeration of a good case. He is free from the silly vanity which spoils so many politicians. He has great charm and a sense of humour.[167]

Dalton identified disunity in the Labor Party in New South Wales, which should have been the stronghold of the Federal Labor Party, as Curtin's biggest problem. If unity could be restored in that key state, Dalton predicted that the ALP would win a sweeping victory in 1940 and Curtin would become prime minister. Already Labor was in power in three of six states: in Western Australia under Philip Collier's successor, John Willcock, a former engine driver; in Queensland under William Forgan Smith, an ex-house painter from Scotland; and in Tasmania, under the brilliant lawyer, Albert Ogilvie. The winning of a majority in the Commonwealth Parliament, Dalton thought, was

well within reach. Dalton described Curtin as not
'isolationist' but a man who thought that the Lyons
Government was being dragged by Britain into a
European war. Australians, Curtin insisted, should
not be committed to war beyond their borders, except
with the consent of the Australian people and with no
conscription for service overseas.[168]

In Europe the British Government led by Neville
Chamberlain continued to pursue a policy of
'appeasement' of Germany and Italy. On 30 September
1938 the British and French governments reached an
agreement in Munich with the German Government
led by Adolf Hitler and the Italian Government
under Benito Mussolini. This agreement permitted
the Germans to annex the Sudetenland in western
Czechoslovakia in the forlorn hope that the rest of
Czechoslovakia would be left alone, and a war in Europe
avoided.[169] The Czech crisis climaxed at the time when
Curtin's 31-year-old mother died. Curtin supported
the Lyons Government in its backing of Chamberlain's
foreign policy.[170] For Curtin, the defence of Australia
was the government's first duty and not entanglement
in a European war.

Towards the end of the 1930s, some commentators felt
that Curtin's conciliatory style of leadership was no
longer suitable for the Labor Party. He had succeeded
in uniting the party. But facing a government that was
increasingly tattered, some thought that he provided a
weak and unadventurous form of leadership too prone
to avoid anything that might divide Labor.[171] If war had
not come, Curtin's position may have been challenged

by someone like Queensland's Premier, Forgan Smith, or perhaps even Tasmania's Ogilvie, if he had not died prematurely. As it turned out, Australia's involvement in the Second World War between 1939 and 1941 saw Curtin transform his leadership and prepare Labor for government. Part of the reason for this transformation was Curtin's membership of a bipartisan Advisory War Council, which would become what historian John Edwards has called "Curtin's school of government".[172]

Curtin, Menzies and the Advisory War Council, 1939–41

By early 1939 Lyons's health was failing, and he was clashing with his young and ambitious deputy, the Attorney-General, Robert Menzies. Born in 1894 in the Victorian town of Jeparit, Menzies studied law at the University of Melbourne and became one of Victoria's leading barristers.[173] After a career in Victorian state politics from 1928 to 1934, he was elected to the Commonwealth Parliament and immediately became Attorney-General and Minister of Industry in the Lyons Government. Although Menzies supported Britain's appeasement policy, he became increasingly disenchanted with Lyons during 1938 and 1939. Matters came to a head on 20 March 1939 when Lyons, under pressure from the Country Party, decided to repeal provisions for pensions in recently passed national insurance legislation.[174] Frustrated by Lyons's vacillation, Menzies resigned from the government and went to the backbench. Curtin seized upon Lyons's retreat from his commitment to introduce a national insurance scheme as evidence of the Lyons Government's impending collapse.[175] Within less than a month, on 7 April, Lyons suffered a heart attack; he died a few days later in hospital on Good Friday.

The UAP was the larger party in a UAP – Country Party coalition but, after Menzies's resignation, it had no deputy. Consequently, Billy Hughes, now the UAP Attorney-General, recommended that the Governor-General should commission Earle Page, the leader of the Country Party and second ranking member of the ministry, as prime minister. This would allow the UAP time to elect a leader.[176] By this time Menzies and Page had developed an intense disliking for each other.[177] Page declared that the Country Party would refuse to serve in a Menzies-led Government. Menzies nevertheless won the leadership, narrowly, in a field of four, defeating Hughes, his closest challenger, by four votes.[178] He formed a government which did not include any Country Party members. Page, before resigning as prime minister, attacked Menzies in the House of Representatives, accusing him of disloyalty to Lyons and criticising his decision not to volunteer to serve in the Australian Imperial Force in the Great War.[179]

In the meantime, Germany had marched into Prague in defiance of the Anglo-French guarantee to Czechoslovakia, dealing Chamberlain's policy of appeasement a fatal blow. On 31 March 1939, the British Government responded with a guarantee of Poland, the next likely target of Hitler's aggression.[180] Germany, nevertheless, applied increasing pressure on Poland. At issue were those clauses of the Treaty of Versailles that had carved out of formerly German territory in Prussia a corridor, giving an otherwise landlocked Poland access to the sea at the free port city of Danzig. By this time, the mood in the British Government had firmed against Germany. On 22 August Chamberlain sent Hitler a letter warning that Britain would stand by its commitment to Poland's sovereignty and independence. But Hitler would not be deterred; he invaded Poland on 1 September.[181]

On 3 September Britain declared war on Germany, and Menzies followed with an announcement on the same day that, "in consequence of the persistence of Germany in her invasion of Poland, Great Britain has declared war upon her, and that, as a result, Australia is also at war".[182] While the Labor Party had sought to resist Australia's entanglement in European affairs in the 1930s, its mood had shifted in reaction to Germany's blatant acts of aggression in Czechoslovakia and Poland (combined with earlier incorporation of Austria in the German Reich). After an interview with Menzies, Curtin stated that the Prime Minister had briefed him fully about the international situation and the predicament of the British Empire. On the following day, 4 September, he articulated Labor's policy on the war: "We stand for the defence of Australia to the greatest degree of which we are capable, and for the maintenance of the British Commonwealth of Nations".[183] In the House of Representatives, on the day after, he declared that Labor would support measures for the "welfare and safety" of the Australian people and the British Commonwealth.[184] Two weeks later, on 15 September 1939, Menzies announced formation of a

War Cabinet, which became the main decision-making body for the "conduct of the war other than matters of major policy".[185] Matters of major policy would be determined by the full cabinet.

In the early stages of the war, Australia had to decide what form of contribution it would make to the British Empire's war effort. Menzies has sometimes been portrayed as too trusting in British strategy, but he was cautious about committing Australian military forces abroad when Japan's continuing neutrality was uncertain.[186] He sent Richard Casey, Minister for Supply, to England to discuss the matter with the British Government. Assisted by Bruce, the Australian High Commissioner in London, Casey negotiated imperial purchase arrangements by which Britain undertook to buy most of the output of key primary industries throughout the war. Casey also brokered an arrangement for Britain to assist in provision to Australia of loan monies to ensure that Australia's international reserves would not be depleted during the war.[187] These negotiations, which substantially satisfied the interests of the Country Party, helped to smooth the path to the Menzies Government's dispatch of an expeditionary force to Europe.

By this time there was a strong popular mood for helping the Mother Country. Menzies agreed to Australia's participation in an Empire Air Training Scheme and dispatch of an army expeditionary force, the second Australian Imperial Force (AIF), to support Britain. Curtin declined to support the decision, maintaining that Australia should build up its home defences and aid Britain's war effort by supplying food and raw materials.[188] He also stood resolutely against conscription for service overseas. At the same time, however, Curtin appreciated the degree of popular support for helping Britain and softened his criticism of the Menzies Government's decision to send the 6th Division AIF abroad in January 1940.[189] The attachment of Australians to Britain was such that, politically, Curtin could not stand completely against the sending of part of Australia's war effort to distant theatres. As it was, his war policy may have cost him winning government in the 1940 election and endangered his own seat. Where he was justified, in 1939 and later, was to have criticised the degree to which Australia depleted its own defences, especially in the air, in support of Great Britain.[190]

In the meantime, the United Kingdom had sent an Expeditionary Force to support France against Germany. The early months of 1940 were dubbed the 'phoney war' because there was only one limited military operation on the Western Front. During this time, some within British Government pressed for a negotiated peace with Germany. Curtin had to tread a fine line again between those in the Labor Party who favoured a negotiated peace and others who wanted to support Britain in its prosecution of the war.[191] The idea of a negotiated peace was eventually scotched by Winston Churchill, who succeeded Neville Chamberlain as Prime Minister of Britain on 10 May 1940. This was when the German armies launched their invasion of Belgium, Luxembourg and France.[192] In the last days of May it seemed that the entire British

Expeditionary Force might be lost to the German onslaught. It was not until the end of the month that the prospect emerged of large-scale evacuation of more than 337,000 troops from Dunkirk that would be eventually carried out by and under direction of the Royal Navy.[193]

On 21 June Marshal Pétain, who had succeeded to the leadership of France, negotiated an armistice with Germany. This allowed him to govern an unoccupied zone in the south of France from the administrative centre of Vichy, and to direct some of the French war effort in the Mediterranean theatre. Following the surrender of France, the Churchill and Menzies governments agreed that Australia's expeditionary force would fight in Britain's Mediterranean, or Middle East, campaign. Its main combat role took place in the large area of the eastern Mediterranean extending from the shores of North Africa eastwards to Greece and westwards from Syria to the toe of Italy. The 6th AIF Division went into action first in January 1941 and was subsequently joined by the 7th and 9th Divisions, who fought several campaigns in North Africa, Greece, Crete, Syria and Lebanon.

Since the Depression, governments in the United Kingdom had been 'national governments', or coalitions of some or all of the major political parties, principal of which was the Conservative party.[194] The British Labour Party Prime Minister, Ramsay MacDonald, formed the first such national government in 1931 and he was succeeded by the leaders of the Conservative Party, first Stanley Baldwin (1935–37) and then

Neville Chamberlain (1937–40), who continued such coalitions.[195] In May 1940, following a political crisis over Britain's botched campaign in Norway, Winston Churchill succeeded Chamberlain and formed a totally restructured national government, including members of the official Opposition, the Labour Party led by Clement Attlee and other Liberals.[196] Churchill thus led a 'national' coalition government consisting of members of all the major parties, the Conservative, Labour and Liberal parties, during the war. Moreover, by agreement between the major political parties, the Westminster Parliament agreed to pass legislation to suspend the conduct of national elections during the war. The House of Commons elected in 1935 thus lasted for ten years.

The idea that something similar might happen in Australia had some attraction for Lyons and Menzies before and during the Second World War. Curtin was against the idea. This was partly because Labor members in the Commonwealth Parliament split again in 1940 and Curtin's joining a 'national' government under Menzies risked further fragmenting the party. Curtin explained to the House of Representatives in 1939 that:

> So long as the people of Australia give to Labor in the Parliament a minority of members, we shall accept the duty cast upon us, that of opposition. But, when the people of Australia, as I hope and think they will, cast on us the responsibility of government, then we shall accept the responsibility on our own policy, a

> policy which the people first have approved, and we shall not be involved in struggles for portfolios and leadership.[197]

Although Curtin had successfully arranged a reconciliation with the 'Langites' in New South Wales in 1936, left-wing forces gained control of the New South Wales branch of the Labor Party in 1939. Many were sympathetic to the Soviet Union, which had signed a non-aggression pact with Germany in the weeks preceding the invasion and dismemberment of Poland, and some even held secret membership of the Communist Party. In 1940 the New South Wales Labor Conference passed a resolution calling for a 'Hands off Russia' policy, widely seen as a policy directed at opposing any Australian involvement in the war.[198] Lang, who notwithstanding his radicalism had always been strongly anti-communist, denounced the policy, seceded from Labor and, on 7 April 1940, announced formation of a new party called the 'Australian Labor Party (Non-Communist)'.[199] In the Commonwealth Parliament, to Curtin's chagrin, seven Labor members joined the breakaway party. Beasley, its chosen leader, had been a key figure in the defeat of the Scullin Government. He was joined by Sol Rosevear, Joe Gander, Dan Mulcahy and Tom Sheehan in the House of Representatives and Stan Amour and John Armstrong in the Senate.[200] Conspicuously absent was Eddie Ward. Only months away from a general election, the split made Curtin's prospect of taking Labor to office much less likely. Curtin lamented that Lang and Beasley had once again stabbed the Labor Party in the back.[201]

To satisfy public pressure for some mechanism to promote greater political harmony during the war, on 22 June 1940 Curtin suggested to Menzies not the formation of a 'National Government' but of a 'National War Council'.[202] This Council, including an equal number of representatives from the Government and the Opposition, would advise the Government on both the conduct of the war and post-war reconstruction.[203] After Menzies sought clarification, Curtin explained that his proposed Council would not be an executive body duplicating the War Cabinet. Rather, it would be an advisory body and a political mechanism to "carry out the war with the greatest speed and efficiency and the least amount of friction".[204] After fully considering Curtin's suggestion in the War Cabinet, Menzies replied to Curtin on 12 July that:

> Cabinet is of opinion that no good purpose would be served by the formation of a National War Council of an advisory kind. To put the matter quite briefly, it feels that an advisory council whose advice is to be worth anything must have knowledge at least equal to that of the Cabinet, and that it is unreasonable that such complete and confidential knowledge should be given to a body which accepts no responsibility for decisions made or action taken.[205]

Menzies countered that the Cabinet was more convinced, after the fall of France, that the British countries of the world had entered the "most critical phase of their history" and that what was necessary for a concerted national war effort was a "national government".[206] He was prepared to offer Labor five or six seats of nineteen ministries, including a new Department of Labour. Menzies went on to implore Curtin:

> Why cannot your people and mine now go the full distance and decide that while this war lasts, they will accept a joint responsibility and exercise a joint authority for the safety and wellbeing of the nation and the building of a better and juster way of life for our future?[207]

After referring the matter to his caucus colleagues, Curtin declined Menzies's initial invitation, which was a rather ungenerous offer to a party with the parliamentary representation and popular support that the Federal Labor Party enjoyed. Thus, the Australian election, prescribed by Section 28 of the Australian Constitution, proceeded under normal arrangements. Any prospect of a bipartisan petition to the British Parliament to expedite suspension of elections for the duration of the war was thus totally ruled out.

As was the case in 1937, Curtin launched his 1940 election campaign from Perth. From there on 28 August 1940, he delivered a speech broadcast throughout Australia. Curtin campaigned for Labor to win.[208] He undertook to lead a Labor government that would prosecute the war actively. At the same time, he cautioned that Australia should prioritise its own defence and not rush to do battle in distant theatres elsewhere in the world. As no Advisory War Council had yet been established, Curtin did not hesitate to charge the Menzies Government with having prosecuted the war inefficiently. He reprised some of his thinking during the Great War when he contended that the Australian Government had to take the longer view and plan for a better peace rather than handing "over the trophies of the new order to profiteers and capitalists".[209] Curtin also cleverly exploited sectional grievances. He promised special assistance for wheat growers and to increase pensions and pay for members of the Australian armed services. Finally, Curtin exploited discontent among automobile and truck drivers occasioned by the Menzies Government's decision to ration petrol.[210]

By way of contrast, Menzies did not make any specific promises. He called for even greater sacrifices for the war effort. During the campaign he publicly reiterated his earlier offer to afford the Labor Party generous representation in an all-party government. David Day has persuasively argued that Menzies's continuing references to an all-party government undermined his larger case that Australia needed a single wartime leader, and that voting Labor would wreck the war effort.[211]

In 1938 Dalton had predicted that Curtin would lead Labor to victory in 1940 if the problems in the New South Wales branch of the party could be fixed. In the 1940 election, however, the New South Wales party was divided between Federal Labor, the Non-Communist Labor Party (the 'Langites') and another group that was basically a front for the Communist Party, which the government had banned in 1940, the Hughes-Evans group or State Labor Party. The split in the New South Wales branch did not augur well for a national Labor victory. Paradoxically, however, New South Wales was the state which gave Labor its major gains. The outcome of the election, held on 21 September 1940, was that the combined representation of the Labor parties from New South Wales in the House of Representatives increased from eleven (six Federal Labor and five 'Langites') to sixteen (twelve Federal Labor and four 'Langites'). Curtin's Federal Labor Party won Reid from Joe Gander, Calare and Riverina from the Country Party, and Watson, Macquarie and Barton from the UAP. Ben Chifley, the former Minister for Defence in the Scullin Government, returned as Member for Macquarie and Herbert Vere Evatt, a former Labor state parliamentarian and High Court judge, won Barton. In Victoria, the Federal Labor Party retained Richard Casey's former seat of Corio, picked up at a by-election by John Dedman, and won Wannon from the UAP; and in Queensland Labor took the rural seat of Maranoa from the Country Party. Taken together, the net gains for the ALP in New South Wales, Victoria and Queensland, were seven seats. This was enough, when added to gains in by-elections between 1937 and 1940, to deliver the Labor Party a majority in the House of Representatives and government.[212]

The problem for Curtin was that the ALP simultaneously lost Wakefield in South Australia and Wilmot in Tasmania—both won in earlier by-elections—and a second Tasmanian seat of Denison. An even more calamitous setback for Labor was that Curtin almost lost Fremantle to the UAP's Frederick

Lee. Curtin had been forced to neglect his constituency by covering nearly 13,000 kilometres in 21 days of campaigning in the eastern states.[213] Immediately after the election, Lee was confident of winning and was preparing to move to Canberra as Fremantle's new representative.[214] For his part, on 23 September, Curtin wrote to the Secretary of the Labor caucus what was tantamount to a resignation letter.[215] As the counting continued, however, Curtin was saved when the preferences of an independent UAP candidate, Gil Clarke, failed to flow in sufficient numbers to Lee and postal votes of soldiers, grateful for Labor's promising them extra pay, went to Curtin.[216] He ultimately defeated Lee with 50.56 per cent of the vote.[217]

The result of this close but indecisive general election was that the Federal Labor and the 'Langites' won 36 seats between them. This was the same number as the combined representation of the UAP and the Country Party in the House of Representatives. The arbiters in this finely balanced house were two Victorian independents: Arthur Coles, elected to the seat of Henty (replacing Sir Henry Gullett killed in an aeroplane crash in Canberra), and Alexander Wilson, who represented the Victorian seat of Wimmera. Both seats won by independents were normally held by the non-Labor parties. In the Senate Labor kept its representation at 16 out of 36 seats.[218]

In these circumstances it was reasonable for Menzies to continue his wartime government and the two Labor parties to form the Opposition. Since March 1940 and Page's replacement as leader of the Country

Party, the Menzies Government was a coalition government between the UAP, led by Menzies, and the Country Party, headed by the South Australian, Archie Cameron, who became *de facto* deputy Prime Minister and Minister for Commerce.[219] When the Country Party tired of Cameron's domineering style, the more easy-going Queenslander Arthur Fadden took the leadership, initially on an acting basis following an intractable split between the veteran Dr Earle Page and relative newcomer from Victoria, John McEwen; Fadden, an accountant, became Treasurer.[220]

For Menzies, a coalition with the Country Party was insufficient to ensure stable government given his fragile majority in the House of Representatives, and he once again approached Curtin to invite him to consider joining a national government.[221] The Minister for the Army, Percy Spender, advised Menzies on 3 October that "[i]t looks on present indications as if we have to depend on the very doubtful support of two independents", making the urgency and importance of renewed discussions with Curtin more obvious.[222] The result of the post-election negotiations between Curtin and Menzies was that Labor declined to join a national government, but Menzies finally relented and agreed to the establishment of an Advisory War Council.[223] The first meeting of the Council on 29 October 1940 consisted of four cabinet ministers, three members of the Federal Labor Party, including Curtin, and Beasley as leader of the 'Langites'.[224] Frederick Shedden, Secretary of the Department of Defence Co-ordination, was Secretary of the War Cabinet and the new Advisory War Council.[225]

Curtin became a valuable and effective member of the Advisory War Council and maintained cordial relations with Menzies in discussions on the administration and disposition of Australia's war effort.[226] The Council helped both major parties to move closer to each other in defence policy and provided Labor members with invaluable political experience. As John Edwards has persuasively argued, Curtin would not have been as strong a prime minister as he was without his experience on the War Council.[227] Notwithstanding his 1937 strategic arguments, Curtin was forced to operate largely within the framework of the Singapore strategy of Imperial defence in 1940 and 1941. In the context of continuing US neutrality, this implied supporting Australia's Middle East commitment in return for promises of British support to reinforce Singapore if the latter were threatened by Japan. For his part, Menzies agreed to enhanced measures for local and regional defence, notably commitment of the 8th AIF Division to reinforce Malaya in 1941. It was partly to press on Churchill the need for more allied resources in Singapore that Menzies made a politically risky mission to Britain from January to May 1941.[228] This lengthy visit, in taking Menzies away from tending his supporters in the House of Representatives, arguably played a large part in Menzies's political downfall and Curtin's rise to power.

Menzies and Curtin both suffered from difficult or disloyal colleagues. In Menzies's case it was a circle of backbenchers around the New South Wales MPs, Bill McCall and Charles Marr, who criticised what they thought to be Menzies's lack of vigour in conducting

Australia's war effort.[229] Some of Menzies's problems with colleagues, however, came from his own inability to suffer fools. Curtin once remarked of him: "Ah, poor Bob, it's very sad; he would rather make a point than make a friend".[230] Curtin had most trouble with Evatt, who chafed at Curtin's caution and schemed with other colleagues, including Beasley and the firebrand Member for East Sydney, Eddie Ward.[231] In December 1940, Evatt rushed to Western Australia in an unsuccessful effort to prop up the Labor candidate in the by-election for the seat of Swan. Later, in May 1941, he undermined Curtin by suggesting to Menzies that some members of the Labor Party might be willing to join a national government when Curtin was continuing to resist the idea.[232] On the other hand, Evatt's candidacy in Barton and his unstinting help for colleagues such as Max Falstein in Watson had contributed to Labor's electoral success in New South Wales in September 1940. John Murphy has also indicated that Evatt was the kind of figure likely to attract middle-class voters otherwise hesitant about Labor.[233]

The Advisory War Council came in useful to both leaders in debate on Menzies's 1940 budget.[234] Curtin formulated his attack on three grounds. He opposed levying income taxation on lower-waged workers; he demanded an increase in old-age and invalid pensions; and he called for more liberal use of central bank credit.[235] When Curtin put up the amendment to the first item in the budget, Menzies feared that the government would be defeated.[236] Curtin, however, saw dangers in taking office at a time when the Labor Party was still divided and having to negotiate with Lang

Labor members and independents. This risked Labor taking office but the new government not lasting more than a few months. He therefore sought a compromise with Menzies in the Advisory War Council. Matters were not helped when Evatt, who was not at that stage on the Council, combined with other Labor 'wild men' to push for defeat of the Menzies Government.[237] Only when Menzies raised the possibility of being forced to advise another election, was Curtin finally able to negotiate a compromise with Menzies involving a face-saving increase in pensions.[238]

In February 1941, with Menzies in England, Curtin made prescient observations about Japan's likely actions in the war.[239] He described Japan's policy as opportunistic and predicted that it would "make war" tomorrow if circumstances were favourable. Japan, he thought, would use its navy to immobilise Australia "with disastrous effect on our commercial and economic life".[240] In addition, he could not overlook the possibility of the temporary occupation by Japan of some portions of Australia. As Australia was dependent on the route through the Indian Ocean for international trade and reinforcement of troops, additional naval forces were urgently needed to reinforce the Australia Station.[241] Curtin recommended that the Menzies Government should put Australia on a "war footing" and encourage mobilisation of both the fighting front and the home front. His aim was to bring home the imminent danger Australia faced to its people.[242] The Acting Prime Minister, Arthur Fadden, appreciated Curtin's support and confided to Menzies that the Labor leader was being particularly helpful in his efforts to dampen down strikes in Australia.²⁴³

In March 1941 Churchill sought the approval of Menzies and his cabinet for Australian military forces to participate in an invasion of Greece, under attack from the Italians and later the Germans also. Both Menzies and the Australian commander in the Middle East, Lieutenant-General Sir Thomas Blamey, feared that the proposed operation was militarily risky and might end in disaster.²⁴⁴ Churchill convinced them that support of Greece was necessary and that the campaign had a reasonable prospect of success.²⁴⁵ In Australia, Curtin and other Labor members of the Advisory War Council declined to reach any decision on Australia's involvement in Greece. They emphasised, however, their party's general disposition that Australian military forces in the Mediterranean theatre should be gradually withdrawn given the threat to Australia from Japan.²⁴⁶

Labor's reservations had no effect, and the invasion of Greece went ahead with the consent of Menzies and the Australian War Cabinet. Australians joined with New Zealand and British forces to defend Greece against a threatened German invasion. The 6th Division arrived in Greece early in April 1941 and on 6 April the Germans commenced their invasion. After a month of intensive fighting, the Allied force had to be evacuated from mainland Greece by sea. Some were taken back to Egypt while others were put ashore on the island of Crete to meet a feared German invasion. The Germans launched a major paratrooper landing at three points on the island on 20 May 1941. In the face of the German assault, the Allied force in Crete, in turn, had to be withdrawn by British and Australian warships. About 39 per cent of the Australian troops in Greece were either killed, wounded or captured as prisoners of war.[247]

Menzies bore the political brunt of the debacle and, after returning to Australia, again approached Curtin and Labor to join a national government.[248] By this time Menzies was being increasingly harassed by backbench malcontents and was also under assault from the *Sydney Morning Herald* and Keith Murdoch's group of newspapers, including the Melbourne *Herald* and *Sun News Pictorial*.[249] Depressed by local politics, Menzies was anxious to return to Britain to sit as Australian Prime Minister in an Imperial War Cabinet. His major objective was to improve the efficiency of Churchill's War Cabinet and ensure that Singapore's defences were strengthened. In doing so, Menzies significantly misjudged not only the Labor Party but also his cabinet colleagues and members of the coalition parties. While Curtin himself was personally amenable to Menzies's return to London (by giving him a pair), his Labor colleagues on the Advisory Council were not.[250] They argued that Menzies's place was in Australia, and Forde even cast doubt on whether Menzies retained the confidence of the House of Representatives.[251] Forde's assessment proved correct as Menzies had now lost the confidence of his cabinet colleagues and his own party room. Refusing Menzies's invitation to join a national government, Curtin advised Menzies on 26 August to resign as prime minister on the assumption that Curtin would be able to lead a Labor minority government that had the confidence of the House of Representatives.[252]

Curtin could be more confident now of the success of such a government because the Federal Labor Party had reunified with the 'Langites' in February 1941.[253] Menzies resigned his commission as prime minister on 28 August 1941, replaced as prime minister by Arthur Fadden. Fadden's war leadership was short-lived. On 3 October the two independents, Wilson and Coles, crossed the floor to support Labor in the budget debate and Fadden was forced to resign. The Governor-General thereupon commissioned Curtin as prime minister and he was sworn in on 7 October 1941. This remains the only time since the introduction of an elected two-party system in 1910 that the Commonwealth government has changed hands because of a parliamentary confidence vote.

While historian Paul Hasluck criticised Curtin for not joining a national government, Curtin was prudent to have resisted Menzies's invitation.[254] His Advisory War Council, moreover, proved to be an effective mechanism for securing a workable parliament in a period of minority government. Critics like Evatt and Beasley at times charged Curtin with having insufficient zeal to defeat the Menzies Government.[255] But to have pushed for government too early, such as in November–December 1940, would have been premature. By waiting until Labor was more unified and until the Menzies and Fadden governments had completely collapsed, he gave himself and Labor a better chance of establishing an effective wartime government with moral legitimacy. Curtin's philosophy of opposition, mixing cautious support for the Australian war effort with improving the position of working people, suited the times.

The Battle for Australia, 1941–43

Shortly after becoming prime minister, Curtin received a letter from Frank Troy, the Western Australian Agent-General in London. Troy warned Curtin that he could not rely indefinitely on the votes of the two independents in the House of Representatives. For Troy there was only one solution to this problem, to stand on his principles and contrive to "get a dissolution at the earliest possible moment".[256] If Curtin delayed, Troy warned, "the very weakness of your numbers in Parliament will encourage opposition and disaffection and in such circumstances time is working against you".[257] This was the sort of advice that Curtin had given to Scullin and Theodore when their policies were being stymied by the Senate and the Commonwealth Bank. With the experience of six years as Leader of the Opposition, Curtin was more cautious and more amenable to negotiation with independents and political adversaries. In this respect he was greatly assisted by his own innovation, the Advisory War Council. Curtin's response to Troy was that "I think you will agree that future action must be decided by circumstances as they arise".[258]

Labor's political position was alleviated somewhat when both the Speaker, Walter Nairn (UAP), and the Chairman of Committees, Jack Prowse (Country Party), agreed to remain in their positions in the House of Representatives, at least until the new Curtin Government's position was under challenge. The UAP and the Country Party were now in disarray—Menzies resigned as UAP leader when his party acquiesced in Fadden becoming Leader of the Opposition. But they remained a powerful force that had only been nudged out of office "rather than overwhelmed on the parliamentary floor".[259] Many in the Opposition remained confident that they would reclaim office and that the Curtin Government would not retain office for more than three months.[260] They had reason to doubt that Labor had the competence to govern in periods of war and crisis considering the Fisher–Hughes governments' experience from 1914 to 1916 and the Scullin Government's unhappy two-year stint from 1929 to 1931.

Even with Nairn as Speaker, the Curtin Government had to rely on the vote of Blackburn, who had been expelled from the Labor Party again in October 1941 for supporting the Australia–Soviet Friendship League, and Labor dissident and former 'Langite' Rowley James. In the upper house, the ALP had 17 Senators, two fewer than the coalition parties' 19 Senators. Consequently, between October 1941 and August 1943, "[n]ot a piece of legislation could be framed by the Cabinet with the certainty that it would be passed in the form in which the Government framed it".[261]

One of Curtin's greatest achievements was to assemble and hold together a ministry that had the confidence of the House of Representatives and could claim to be more than a stopgap. This was even more of an accomplishment given that only four members of the new government had ministerial experience of any sort: Forde, Chifley, Beasley and Holloway. Like Menzies, Curtin took the additional portfolio of Defence Co-ordination (Defence from 14 April 1942). He transformed himself completely in government.[262] Lloyd Ross, one of Curtin's biographers wrote: "From the day that Curtin became Prime Minister, his personality seemed to change. He walked confidently. No longer neurotic nor lackadaisical, he grew determined and ruthless in enforcing his basic ideas".[263] The *Sydney Morning Herald* agreed, dubbing him a "miraculously changed person".[264] For historian of the Commonwealth Parliament, Gavin Souter, "Curtin was a patient and resourceful parliamentary tactician—perhaps, it has been said, the best manager of an evenly divided parliament since Deakin".[265]

Curtin's deputy, the colourless but loyal Frank Forde, became a competent Minister for the Army and served as Curtin's Deputy Prime Minister for the duration of the war. Curtin's ministry was, however, essentially dominated by four ministers: Curtin, Chifley, Evatt, and Beasley.[266] Aside from the 'big four', the ministry had a long tail with many ministers chosen for seniority rather than competence. Exceptions were Arthur Drakeford, Minister for Air and Civil Aviation, William Scully, the Minister for Commerce and Agriculture, and John Dedman, the Minister for War Organisation of Industry.

According to historian John Nethercote, Curtin was the first Australian prime minister to relinquish the day-to-day responsibilities of Leader of the House of Representatives.[267] These responsibilities he delegated to Chifley, whom Curtin also appointed Treasurer. Chifley proved to be a "masterly controller of business", meticulously working out a legislative programme at the beginning of each parliamentary session, mapping each day's work with the Clerk of the House, keeping a close watch on the preparation of bills, and affording ready access to the Leader of the Opposition, Fadden, in the management of parliamentary business.[268]

The tireless and relentless Evatt became Attorney-General and Minister for External Affairs and succeeded Chifley as Leader of the Federal Parliamentary Labor Party in 1951. In government Curtin was able to establish a *modus vivendi* with Evatt.[269] This involved sometimes reining him in but also harnessing his obvious political and legal talents.[270] Beasley joined the War Cabinet to become an able Minister for Supply and Development (Supply and Shipping from October 1942), and Curtin's old friend, Holloway, took on the Ministry for Social Services and Health. On joining the cabinet, Beasley transformed completely, thereafter remaining steadfastly loyal to Curtin.[271]

Against Curtin's wishes, caucus elected the firebrand New South Welshmen, Eddie Ward, to the ministry. Ward remained a thorn in Curtin's side arising from his vendetta against the Menzies Government for its ostensible advocacy of a defeatist strategy of defending Australia against a Japanese invasion south of the so-called 'Brisbane Line'. He proved to be a competent Minister for Labour and National Service but would lose that portfolio to Holloway in 1943 when Arthur Calwell, another critic of Curtin, also joined the ministry as Minister for Information.²⁷² John Dedman, a Scot and war veteran, who had migrated to Australia in 1922, became Minister for War Organisation of Industry. The Depression years had radicalised Dedman to become a staunch advocate for government control of the economy and he too became an able ally for Curtin as well as a capable administrator.²⁷³ On 7 November 1941 Curtin announced formation of a Production Executive or economic committee of Cabinet, chaired by Dedman and appointed Essington Lewis, the managing director of the Broken Hill Proprietary Company, as Director-General of Aircraft Production as well as Munitions.²⁷⁴

Success of the Curtin Government depended on more than one man. Curtin had a powerful core of senior ministers and able public servants to support the weaker ministers. Among these public servants were recently recruited officials such as Hebert Cole 'Nugget' Coombs, appointed Director of Rationing in 1942 and Director-General of the Department of Post-War Reconstruction in 1943, and Roland Wilson, who had become Secretary of the Department of Labour and National Service under Menzies in 1940. These were two of a remarkable group of mandarins that came to be known as the 'seven dwarfs'.²⁷⁵ In addition to these senior public servants, Curtin came to depend on Chifley to manage the economy and parliamentary business, on Evatt for advice on legal, constitutional and some international matters, and on Shedden, the Secretary of the Department of Defence, in the realm of military and strategic affairs.[275] Moreover, he developed, as will be seen, a close, and some have argued, overly dependent relationship with the US General, Douglas MacArthur. Nonetheless, Curtin remained *primus inter pares* in a ministry forced to deal with the most extraordinary crisis in Australia's history. The circumstances of the war gave Curtin, as they gave Winston Churchill, no other choice than to delegate some important functions of government to concentrate on matters of defence and allied strategy.[277] Curtin remained the key minister responsible for strategic and military affairs, displayed an extraordinary ability to manage the press and remained the dominant parliamentary performer in a House of Representatives that included another formidable rhetorician, Robert Menzies.[278] Over time Curtin also managed to transcend his position as leader of a party to become an inspirational national figure.

After Japan attacked the United States naval base at Pearl Harbor on 7 December 1941, the Curtin Government had to confront Australia's gravest national crisis. On 8 December, Curtin opened his radio broadcast to the nation with the words: "Men and Women of Australia. We are at war with Japan".[279] The speech ended with a call to mobilise, using the poetry of Swinburne:

> Come forth, be born and live,
> Thou that hast help to give,
> And light to make man's day of manhood fair;
> With flight outflying the sphered sun,

> Hasten thine hour
> And halt not til thy work be done.[280]

The Japanese attack brought the hitherto neutral United States into the war, but this was a war that it waged on two fronts. President Franklin D. Roosevelt quickly agreed with Churchill that the defeat of Germany must take priority over the war against Japan. Britain had fought off a threatened German invasion of the British Isles in 1940 and 1941 and was now heavily engaged in the Mediterranean theatre. Nonetheless, Churchill did send the prized British battleship *HMS Prince of Wales* and the battlecruiser *HMS Repulse* to relieve Singapore.[281] Disastrously for the allied war effort they were sunk by Japanese aircraft two days after Pearl Harbor. This left Australia with three of its best AIF divisions in the Middle East and most of its Air Force in Britain. Australia was consequently ill-prepared to resist a Japanese attack, lacking modern fighter aircraft, tanks and aircraft carriers. Curtin insisted that the British Government should continue to make good its promises to reinforce Singapore.

At the same time, he made overtures to Australia's new ally in the Pacific, the United States. On 27 December 1941 Curtin announced dramatically in a new year's message prepared for a Melbourne newspaper that:

> The Australian Government ... regards the Pacific struggle as primarily one in which the United States and Australia must have the fullest say in the direction of the democracies' fighting plan. Without any inhibitions of any kind, I make it clear that Australia looks to America, free of any

pangs as to our traditional links or kinship with the United Kingdom.[282]

Curtin's call to America was accompanied by a sense that Australia needed to become more independent and self-reliant. Many, however, saw the phrase 'free of any pangs' as disloyal to the Mother Country. In 1939 Menzies had taken the view that when the King, on the advice of his British ministers, declared war on Germany, the Dominion of Australia was automatically at war. Curtin made it clear that he would not be following Menzies's practice when it came to declaring war on countries like Romania and Japan. With Evatt's support, Curtin insisted on a procedure by which the King would declare war on those countries on behalf of Australia on the advice of Australian ministers. Accordingly, Bruce was advised that:

> ... it is desirable to express with clarity the unbroken chain of prerogative authority from His Majesty to his representative here [the Governor-General], making it also clear at the same time that in relation to the Commonwealth and its Territories, His Majesty is acting exclusively on the advice of his Ministers in the Commonwealth [of] Australia.[283]

The Japanese, now formally at war with Australia, went on to invade the Philippines, to seize Ambon and Rabaul and begin the attack on the British naval base in Singapore. Learning that some in the British Government were considering evacuating Malaya and Singapore, Curtin cabled Churchill on 23 January 1942. He remonstrated to Churchill, in words probably drafted by Evatt:

> After all the assurances we have been given, the evacuation of Singapore would be regarded here and elsewhere as an inexcusable betrayal. Singapore is a central fortress in the system of Empire and local defence ... we understood it was to be made impregnable and in any event it was to be capable of holding out for a prolonged period until the arrival of the main fleet.[284]

Singapore could not hold out against the Japanese Army which attacked the city through Malaya. The Battle for Singapore was joined from 8 to 15 February 1942. The Japanese victory was decisive, resulting in the largest British surrender in its history. Approximately 120,000 British, Indian and Australian personnel were captured. Australians made up the largest proportion of the 5,000 who were killed or wounded in the battle and numbered 15,000 of those taken as prisoners-of-war by the Japanese.[285] Curtin described the fall of Singapore as "Australia's Dunkirk" and suggested that it would be followed by the "Battle for Australia".[286] Four days later, the Japanese invaded Timor, and in successive raids their air force destroyed much of Darwin as well as the ships in its harbour. Curtin told Australians now that there was "no more looking away now. Fate has willed our position in this war".[287]

Some historians have argued that Australia, under Curtin's leadership, faced the real possibility of invasion for the first time in its history.[288] Others, such as Peter Stanley and David Horner, question that the Japanese Government had the intention of invading mainland Australia in 1942.[289] What is common to both sides of the debate is that Japan, through its occupation of Southeast Asia, its invasion of Papua and New Guinea and its capacity to blockade, posed the most significant strategic threat that Australia had faced in its history. In this climate, the Curtin Government introduced unprecedented control over the lives of Australians.

It now became urgently necessary to build roads and airfields in isolated and sparsely populated northern Australia. Imperative, too, was the need to build defence installations around Australia's coastline and barricades on beaches and to prepare plans to demolish ports and harbours in the event of Japanese attack. To carry out these tasks, Curtin created an Allied Works Council to oversee construction projects at home and abroad. Edward 'Ted' Theodore, in business since the loss of his political career in 1931, became its Director-General, with the power to acquire property compulsorily and to spend up to £250,000 without prior approval.[290] The Curtin Government also set up a Civil Constructional Corps, consisting of both volunteers and conscripts, to provide a workforce for the Allied Works Council.

The Curtin Government tightened restrictions on consumption, trade, employment, supply and travel, raised taxation rates, prohibited manufacture of unnecessary commodities and introduced an identity card to supplement the passport. In effect, Curtin put the whole of the nation's productive system under government control and suspended many of the incentives that normally operate under a market system. He gave responsibility for controlling and directing the economy to one of its standing committees, the Production Executive, chaired by Dedman as Minister for War Organisation of Industry.[291] In so mobilising Australia for total war, Paul Hasluck has persuasively argued that Curtin faced a longer and harder challenge than the task of assembling the war effort that was carried out by Menzies between 1939 and 1941.[292]

To meet the feared invasion of Australia, Curtin resolved to bring the AIF Divisions back to Australia as quickly as possible. Before Singapore's fall, Churchill had agreed that the 6th and 7th Divisions should be diverted either to defend Singapore or to safeguard the Netherlands East Indies (modern day Indonesia), while the 9th Division remained, at least for a time, in the Middle East. After the fall of Singapore and forced allied evacuation of Java, Churchill then pressed Curtin to allow the troopships carrying the 7th Division AIF to be diverted to defend Burma.[293] Curtin's defence advisers, including Lieutenant General Vernon Sturdee, stressed to Curtin that both divisions were necessary to defend Australia and should come back to Australia. Unfortunately for Curtin, Churchill enlisted the help of Roosevelt to persuade Curtin to allow diversion of the 7th Division to Burma for the greater good of the allied war effort against Japan. In Roosevelt's view the defence of Burma was vitally important to bolster Chiang Kai-shek's resistance to the Japanese in China.

Backed by his defence advisers, Curtin stood firm against Churchill and Roosevelt and insisted on the return to Australia of both divisions. Menzies and the Opposition parties in Canberra as well as Australia's envoys, Earle Page, sent to London in 1941 as resident minister in the United Kingdom, Stanley Melbourne Bruce the High Commissioner in London, and Richard Casey, Australia's Minister in Washington, all supported Churchill and Roosevelt against Curtin.[294] The dispute reflected in stark terms the division between those backing an imperial conception of Australia's role in the war and Curtin's view of the paramountcy of national defence within a larger imperial and allied effort. In the end, Churchill had to acquiesce in return of the forces to Australia. Curtin for his part compromised by allowing two brigades to go to Ceylon (modern Sri Lanka) to help prepare that colony for an invasion that never came. It took several months for the troopships to sail across the now perilous waters of the Indian Ocean. Worried lest any harm come to the men, Curtin spent many sleepless nights; to relieve his stress he would sometimes call on his driver, Ray Tracey, for a late-night game of billiards or just a "yarn".[295] Fortunately, the 6th and 7th Divisions returned to Australia unscathed while the 9th Division began embarking for its return to Australia in January 1943.

In March 1942, one month after the fall of Singapore, Roosevelt ordered General Douglas MacArthur, commander of US forces in the Philippines, to organise Pacific defence with Australia.[296] For his part, Curtin agreed to place all of Australia's forces under MacArthur's command and to cede overall responsibility for strategic decision-making to the

American general to whom Roosevelt gave the title Supreme Commander of the South West Pacific. So began the partnership between Curtin and MacArthur with the latter suggesting that Curtin "take care of the rear and I will handle the front".[297] Curtin also sent Evatt to Washington and London to obtain additional personnel and equipment to defend Australia. Evatt discovered that Churchill and Roosevelt had agreed on the "beat Hitler first" strategy without consulting Australia.[298] While Evatt was abroad, another irritant to Anglo-Australian relations developed when Churchill decided to appoint Richard Casey, Australia's Minister to the United States since 1940, as British Minister of State for the Middle East with a seat in the British War Cabinet.[299] This disappointed Curtin who pointed out to Casey that:

> We would regard it as a serious disadvantage to Australia if at this point we lose the benefit of the many contacts you have made in the American administration and public life over the past two years, together with your own familiarity which you have acquired as Minister with the many urgent and weighty matters now current in our relationship with the United States.[300]

Some historians have viewed the Curtin–MacArthur relationship, which lasted approximately three years, as an effective one. According to this interpretation, Curtin accepted MacArthur as Australia's main military adviser and sought to use him as a conduit to seek greater allied resources for the defence of Australia.[301] For his part, MacArthur appreciated

Curtin's giving him a stable political environment and a means by which MacArthur could press the Roosevelt Administration for more military resources for his command.

Other historians have painted a less rosy picture. The military historian, Gavin Long, argued that the Curtin Government "had made a notable surrender of sovereignty" when "no Australian Government would have so completely surrendered control of its forces in its own territory to a British commander and staff".[302] In Long's view, this resulted in the Curtin Government having virtually no share in strategic decisions notwithstanding that for the first twelve months it contributed at least the "greater part" of the forces under the South West Pacific Command.[303] MacArthur was late to value the quality of Australia's front-line soldiers and initially and unfairly disparaged them as "no good in the jungle", drawn from the "slums of the cities in Australia" and lacking any "fighting spirit".[304]

During 1942, while American forces in Australia steadily increased, they did not exceed the number of Australian forces. Curtin and MacArthur relied on Australians to bear the brunt of the Japanese assault in Australia's Near North. Although Curtin feared an invasion of Australia, the Japanese decided instead to isolate Australia through a strategy involving the seaborne assault of Port Moresby, administrative centre of Australia's territories of Papua and New Guinea. With intelligence of this move, the US Navy foiled the assault through an engagement with the Japanese Navy in the Battle of the Coral Sea in the first week of May 1942. In the following month, the US Navy fought an even more decisive engagement, the Battle of Midway, sinking four Japanese aircraft carriers.[305]

Their Navy irreparably damaged, the Japanese changed strategy to launch a land attack across the Owen Stanley Ranges on Port Moresby. At MacArthur's request, Curtin sent the Australian army commander, Blamey, to Port Moresby to take personal charge of its defence. After an eight-week Australian offensive on the Kokoda Track and defeat of Japanese forces at Milne Bay, the Japanese assault was finally halted. In November 1942 the Japanese Army turned its attention from Papua and New Guinea to defence of the Solomon Islands base at Guadalcanal. Thereafter, Australian and US troops went on the offensive, attacking heavily fortified beachheads at Gona, Buna and Sanananda.

A second question about Curtin's relationship with MacArthur is how far the latter influenced Australia's home front and particularly how much he influenced Curtin on the question of conscription. By 1942 Curtin had become uncomfortable with the fact that American conscripts were fighting and even dying in Australia's defence while Australia eschewed the idea of conscription for overseas service. In such circumstances, he believed, insistence on retaining conscripts at home had become insupportable. Paul Hasluck, in the official history, argues that the decision to introduce a form of conscription was Curtin's alone. Hasluck's view was that

> [t]here appears to be no evidence, other than rumours current during the controversy,

that either MacArthur or the United States Government had suggested or sought "conscription" of the Australian militia, nor is there any evidence that Australian military advisers had recommended it to the Government.[306]

Other historians such as Peter Love, however, have argued that MacArthur directly "precipitated the move".[307] Love cited confidential transcripts of briefings that Curtin gave to the press. These briefings usually consisted of Curtin "relaxing in a swivel chair, lighting a cigarette ... and 'thinking out loud' (his A.J.A. badge on his watch-chain)."[308] In one of them, on 20 November 1942, Curtin reported that MacArthur had asked him to create "one army" from the members of the Australian Imperial Force, who had volunteered for service abroad and the members of the Citizen Military Forces (the militia), whose members were not liable for overseas service by the *Defence Act* 1903.[309]

Curtin appealed to the bureau heads in Australia by disclosing that the request had come from MacArthur but that he did not want this publicly known because "technically MacArthur should have no concern with a political matter".[310] This was a clever move on Curtin's part. To have attributed the "one army" initiative directly to Curtin would have exposed him to political criticism from the UAP – Country Party Opposition and the full fury of anti-conscriptionist members of his own party. The former would have castigated Curtin for not sending conscripts to New Guinea without the imprimatur of the Labor Party machine. The latter would have accused Curtin of betraying a principle on which he had gone to gaol in 1916.

Curtin's tactics worked superbly. No newspaper publicised MacArthur's involvement. A Special Federal Conference of the ALP in January 1943 gave Curtin the result he wanted, and he proceeded to introduce the *Defence (Citizen Military Forces) Bill* under which members of the militia (including conscripts) would be required to serve in any area of General MacArthur's command in the South West Pacific Area. Introduction of even such a limited form of conscription for overseas service, nonetheless, upset many in the Labor Party. Eddie Ward accused Curtin in caucus of "putting young men into the slaughterhouse although thirty years ago you wouldn't go yourself".[311] More embarrassingly, Arthur Calwell spoke against conscription in the House of Representatives to the delight of the Opposition.[312] But Curtin managed the issue with such dexterity that he avoided a major split in the Labor Party. Whether even such limited conscription was worth the fight, however, is debatable given that the rapid growth in Australia's armed forces in 1942 had already unbalanced the war effort. As Stuart Macintyre has observed, more than anything the decision reflected the relationship of mutual dependence between Curtin and MacArthur in 1942.[313]

The exigencies of war allowed Curtin to bring about significant change to the character of Australian federalism through introduction of uniform taxation of income in 1942.[314] Since the Great War, both the Commonwealth and the states taxed incomes. The competition between the two levels of government for this field of taxation was tolerated during the interwar period but ran into serious problems after 1939. This was because financing the war effort necessitated raising unprecedentedly large amounts from income taxation and because the Commonwealth's efforts to do so were "stultified by the existing tax structure, with its enormous variations in rates and incidence between states".[315]

In 1941, Fadden as Treasurer tried unsuccessfully to persuade the states to suspend their collection of income taxes. When the Curtin Government took office, it was determined to cut the Gordian Knot represented by dual taxation of income. In May 1942 Chifley introduced a series of bills that made it almost impossible for the states to levy income taxes for the duration of the war. The legislation, while not forbidding state taxation outright, stipulated that any state that continued to levy income taxes would have its share of reimbursement grants paid by the Commonwealth reduced by an equivalent sum. That this occurred in wartime did not impress the states who saw it as an attack on 'states' rights'. They soon mounted a challenge to the legislation in the High Court. Brian Galligan, a political scientist, has argued that the High Court's decision in the *Uniform Tax* case "is inexplicable outside the war setting".[316] The Governor-General gave his assent to the bills after the Battle of Midway, in June 1942, and the Court considered the case during a time of national crisis.

The High Court upheld the right of the Commonwealth

to assume such powers under emergency wartime legislation. Menzies opposed the way that the Curtin Government achieved it as in substance a scheme to deprive the states of their taxing powers. Billy Hughes, Leader of the UAP and Deputy Leader of the Opposition and long a centralist, rejoiced that "[t]he States are now relegated to being subordinate legislators as most people want them to be". [317] When the war ended, the Commonwealth did not return the power to tax incomes to the states. Instead, legislation in 1946 made the Commonwealth's control permanent. Hasluck commented that thus a "major change in constitutional relationships and in the political structure of Australia had been made without any formal amendment of the Constitution".[318]

Another major constitutional change was adoption of the *Statute of Westminster* that confirmed the Australian Parliament's legislative independence. In 1931 the passage of the *Statute of Westminster* by the UK Parliament ended subordination of the legislatures of the self-governing dominions to the Parliament at Westminster. The states, however, had mounted vociferous opposition to this imperial self-denying ordinance, and Scullin had been forced to offer them a compromise. He promised the states that the British legislation would only come into force in Australia when it was adopted by the Commonwealth Parliament after consultation with the states. For a decade the states resisted the Commonwealth's adoption of the legislation until, in September–October 1942, the Curtin Government had the Commonwealth Parliament adopt the *Statute of Westminster*, ostensibly to remove doubts as to whether the Australian parliament could legislate extra-territorially in wartime.[319] It is hard to imagine that a UAP – Country Party government would ever have introduced this measure in wartime when it could be construed, an many did construe it, as Australia asserting greater independence from the British Empire. The Commonwealth Parliament did become independent of the Westminster Parliament because of the legislation, although the legislatures of the states, to which the *Statute of Westminster* did not apply, retained their existing relationship to the mother Parliament, a legacy of their former status as colonies. The Curtin Government thus reinforced the sense that Australia had transcended its 'dominion status' provided by its earlier insistence on Australia's separate declaration of war on Japan.[320]

The 1943 Election and Post-war Reconstruction

From about the middle of 1943 Australia's war policy became increasingly uncertain. The main problem for the Curtin Government was how to allocate resources between the armed services and industry, which was also providing food for Britain and supplies for American and British troops. Hasluck argued that the "central feature of the whole manpower situation [was] a constant uncertainty regarding the exact nature of the Australian war effort".[321] For the official historians of the war economy, Sydney Butlin and Boris Schedvin, the Curtin Government's predicament arose because "an important part of the problem which could not be readily resolved was MacArthur's domination of

Curtin".[322] The military historian David Horner agrees, contending that in mid-1943 MacArthur persuaded Curtin to retain a higher number of Australians in front-line services for many months longer than was necessary given that the invasion scare had passed.[323] Putting these views together, the diplomatic historian Peter Edwards has argued that Curtin was "overwhelmed by the demands of wartime leadership and unqualified to take on the role of the strong civilian leader who could command the generals and defend the national interest".[324] Accepting that Curtin may have surrendered more sovereignty to MacArthur than was necessary, such an assessment ignores the heroic efforts that Curtin made to mobilise the home front while keeping the Labor movement united.

In the end, too, the Curtin Government was able to balance the military and civilian sectors. By June 1944, it arranged to release 20,000 men from the army and 20,000 men and women from munitions and aircraft production, and it did not replace normal wastage in the army, which amounted to 76,000 men in 1944. The manpower so diverted was able to help Australia produce more food and resources for the allied war effort. Curtin justified the decision to scale down Australia's military manpower to his allies by pointing out that Australia, with only 66 per cent of its normal labour force, was producing food for 12 million people. This enabled Australia to supply 90 per cent of the needs of US forces in the South West Pacific as well as to supplement New Zealand's supplies to the forces of the South Pacific. Indeed, the value of reciprocal aid to Americans covering all classes of supplies and services was about £100 million in 1943–44, or one-sixth of war expenditure.³²⁵ This system of *de facto* barter greatly assisted the Curtin Government in financing Australia's war effort.

Curtin had managed to steer the government without any turbulence in Parliament. But by June 1943, the patience of the anti-Labor forces with the Curtin Government was wearing thin. The conservative side of Australian politics, although disorganised, had some hopes of defeating Curtin's Government on the floor of the House or at an election. In response to the perceived failures of the aged leader of the UAP, Billy Hughes, a 'National Service Group' was formed inside the party early in 1943.³²⁶ The underlying aim of the group, which supported universal military service in contrast to the limited form of conscription introduced by Curtin in January 1943, was to reorganise and revitalise the UAP and reinstate Menzies as its leader.

In 1943 Curtin's Government faced growing criticism from the press. With strikes increasing, the Sydney *Sun* went as far as issuing an ultimatum to the Curtin Government to "rule the country or give way to men who will".³²⁷ Curtin himself came under personal criticism for not disavowing Eddie Ward's contention that the Menzies Government had backed the 'Brisbane Line'. This referred to an alleged stratagem of abandoning all of Australia north of a line near the Tropic of Capricorn in the event of a Japanese invasion.³²⁸ On 22 June 1943 Fadden moved a censure motion against the Curtin Government; Menzies was the other main speaker for the Opposition. As he had long foreshadowed, Nairn resigned as Speaker and voted with the Opposition; the Government nevertheless survived by one vote.[329] Bowing to the inevitable, on 24 June, Curtin informed the House:

> In my view this Parliament has about exhausted its resources for constructive legislation. I believe that it must be palpable to everyone that when we have passed the necessary measures in relation to carrying on of His Majesty's services ... the question of the capacity of this Parliament to continue to serve the country might be submitted to a higher tribunal.[330]

The Governor-General dissolved the House of Representatives for a general election on 21 August; a periodical election for half the Senate was scheduled for the same day.

Labor entered the campaign with only 36 of the 74 members in the House of Representatives and the Opposition had a four-seat advantage in the Senate. The Labor Party was nervous about the outcome especially when recalling Curtin's narrow escape from defeat in Fremantle in 1940.[331] For that reason, Curtin spent the whole of the last week of the campaign on the hustings in Perth. Before that, on 26 July, he opened his campaign from a radio studio in Canberra to emphasise his role as national leader.[332] He pointed to Labor's war record and mistakes he believed that his predecessors had made before Japan entered the war. But he also stressed the importance of "Australia's membership of the British Commonwealth" and "loyalty to the throne".[333] Curtin campaigned more vigorously early on than in either of the two previous elections to buy him extra time in Perth. This involved his flying in a Lancaster bomber from Adelaide to Perth in what was only the second flight of his life. As the campaign went on, he increasingly emphasised that he was a 'national' rather than a party leader.[334] His appearances in the West largely concentrated on campaigning in Fremantle, including a speech in the Town Hall on 18 August when he made the self-denying promises that the "Labour government would not, during the war, socialise any industry".[335]

Fadden, the Leader of the Opposition, opened his election campaign on 22 July 1943. He recommended forming one army out of the AIF and the Militia. He also urged review of wartime restrictions and regulations and proposed a method of financing the war by levying compulsory loans to be paid back after the war. More generally, Fadden charged the Curtin Government with being in thrall to socialist theories and being unable to resolve industrial disputes.[336]

One theme of the campaign was the disruptiveness of the Australian Communist Party to the war effort. According to historian Hal G. P. Colebatch, unions influenced by Australian Communists systematically sabotaged Australian troops throughout the war.[337] For others, including Hasluck, there were many reasons behind the industrial disputation during the war than the purely ideological.[338] The Australian Communist Party was supportive of the war effort after Germany's invasion of the Soviet Union in June 1941, and the Curtin Government worked hard with union leaders, including Communist leaders of militant unions, to moderate union demands and increase productivity. Nonetheless, on one occasion during the election, Fadden went as far as proposing to ban the Communist Party, a point on which he agreed with Menzies. Menzies, still a private member, spoke on the night after Fadden and repudiated his colleague's proposal for post-war credits. Fadden called this an act of treachery, and a 'stab in the back', an allegation supported by Hughes, who was still formally the Leader of the UAP.[339]

It was clear even before counting ended, that Curtin had led the Labor Party to its most emphatic national victory. Allan Martin, a biographer of Menzies, noted that "deluge" was the word "most often on the lips" of the Opposition and their supporters when the results came in.[340] Labor increased its representation to 49 of the 75 seats in the House of Representatives, more than twice as many as the 23 seats won by the coalition parties together. New South Wales again sustained Labor's success; there Labor's representation increased from 16 to 21 seats, leaving only seven in the hands of the coalition parties. Labor won the seats of Eden-Monaro, Martin, Parkes and Robertson from the UAP and Hume from the Country Party.[341]

The other jewel in Labor's crown was Western Australia. In 1940 Labor had won only two lower house seats: Kalgoorlie and Fremantle, and the latter by a hair's breadth. Three years later, Curtin led Labor to a clean sweep of all Western Australia's seats in the House of Representatives for the first time in history.

Labor's gains included Swan and Forrest, won from the Country Party, and the seat of Perth, in which Curtin had been so badly defeated in 1919. In 1943 Tom Burke won it from the former Speaker, Walter Nairn, with a 20 per cent swing. In his own seat of Fremantle, Curtin polled 67 per cent of the primary votes. South Australia was another good state for Labor. Having won only one of South Australia's six seats in 1940, Labor this time captured another four, Adelaide, Boothby, Grey and Wakefield, leaving Archie Cameron in Barker as the only coalition member.[342] But Labor's gains elsewhere in Australia were more modest, reflecting its stronger performance in other states in 1940. In the Senate, however, Labor's representation rose to 18, or half that chamber from August 1943, and to 21 out of 36 Senators from 1 July 1944. This meant that from July 1944 Labor had majorities in both houses of parliament. Labor's ascendancy was only partly a result of the chaos in the non-Labor parties. Its landslide victory in 1943 also reflected that Labor's political philosophy was more consistent than those of the non-Labor parties with the controlled economy that had become necessary during the Pacific War.

The Curtin Government had begun its preparations for the post-war peace early. To that end, some ministers, like Chifley and Evatt, were keen to hold a referendum for changes to the Constitution to allow the Curtin Government to implement its program for social and economic reconstruction. In 1942 Evatt drafted a *Constitutional Alteration (War Aims and Reconstruction) Bill* to endow the Commonwealth with sweeping but time-limited powers to pursue such allied war aims as had been agreed by Churchill and Roosevelt in their declaration of the Atlantic Charter in August 1941.[343] At that stage of the war, in 1942, a referendum as radical as this held some prospect of success, but Curtin, like Hughes in the Great War, yielded to the wish of the premiers who undertook to persuade their parliaments to refer powers necessary for post-war reconstruction to the Commonwealth. The decision partly reflected Curtin's longstanding adherence to the federal concept and his disposition that what was needed was adjustment of responsibilities between Commonwealth and the states, not a movement in the direction of unification.

Curtin's decision to proceed by co-operation with the states ended in failure. When most states declined to transfer these powers, the Curtin Government in August 1944 submitted a referendum, the *Constitution Alteration (Postwar Reconstruction and Democratic Rights Act) 1944*, to the Australian people. The referendum sought, on an all-or-nothing basis, transfer of fourteen powers to the Commonwealth Government for a period of five years after the war ended.

Some of these constitutional powers, such as civil aviation and uniformity of rail gauges, were uncontroversial. Others, like price control and production and distribution of goods, were politically divisive. Menzies, by now leader of the UAP and Leader of the Opposition, argued that they were not necessary, and that Labor would use them to trample on the liberties of citizens.[344] Aided by Fadden and sympathetic elements of the media, he conjured up a vision of indefinite perpetuation of austerity and implementation of socialisation, which was indeed realised after the war when the Chifley Labor Government tried to nationalise the banks in 1947.[345] Demoralised by the campaign, Curtin "seemed lifeless and disheartened and during the final week of the campaign disappeared altogether from the platform with the flu".[346] A clear overall majority and majorities in four of the states voted 'No'; only in South Australia and Curtin's home state of Western Australia was there a 'Yes' majority.[347]

The defeat of the fourteen powers referendum has sometimes been portrayed as a watershed moment in the move for economic and social reform in the 1940s. It ensured that the task of post-war reconstruction would be more difficult and more protracted, and it made it easier for opponents to mobilise against the Labor's reform agenda. The Labor governments under Curtin and then under Chifley were, nonetheless, able to put many wartime economic controls on a firm peacetime footing without the need for additional constitutional powers. For example, national control of banking, long urged by Curtin, was first introduced under national security regulations, and was later passed into law in 1945 under the Constitution's banking power.[348] Curtin, unlike Chifley, had no aspirations for the nationalisation of industries such as banking. For Curtin, as for long-time Queensland Premier Forgan Smith, national control sufficed. Nonetheless, the experience of the Great Depression had convinced Curtin and his colleagues that governments could and should use all the means at their disposal to achieve full employment. Accordingly, on his return from overseas in 1944, Curtin ordered a group of economists, including 'Nugget' Coombs, to produce a *White Paper on Full Employment in Australia.* Published in 1945, it exercised a powerful influence on official economic policy in Australia until 1975.[349]

Partly under the leadership of Menzies but more so under Curtin, the war, reinforcing developments stemming from the Depression years and the impact of Keynesian demand management economics, transformed the role and power of national government. The public servant and political scientist, Fin Crisp, demonstrated this point with his analysis of the Commonwealth Treasury. Before the war, its primary role was simply to do the Commonwealth's housekeeping and balance the budget. In Treasury speeches in the interwar period matters such as loan raisings and tax revenues were indicators of the economy's health but not instruments for its regulation. Because of the war, the Treasury moved into the centre of a "new process of wide-ranging governmental command of the national economy as a whole".[350] After the conflict, Crisp wrote, the Treasury,

> ... has in itself, in response to various currents and pressures, transcended federal theory and become, under Cabinet, the regulator and, in measure, also the architect of the general contours of the "public sector" as a whole.[351]

The Commonwealth Public Service was another area where great changes occurred because of the war. Mobilisation of hundreds of thousands of Australians, regulation of a war economy and implementation of Labor's plans for war and reconstruction generated the need for a new class of professionals, although graduates had entered the Commonwealth Public Service in greater numbers in the 1930s. The departments of Post-war Reconstruction, External Affairs, Commerce and Agriculture, the Treasury and the Prime Minister's Department were all examples of a shift towards a new professionalism and an influx of university-educated staff during and after the war.[352] Consciousness of the need for an educated professional population was not confined to the Commonwealth Public Service. Under the *Education Act 1945*, passed after Curtin's death, veterans of the war were funded by the Commonwealth to be educated to all levels, including universities; the Australian National University was founded in 1946 as a focus for research excellence within Australia in the service of national interests.[353]

During the war, Curtin forged a close relationship with the Governor-General, Lord Gowrie.[354] In 1943, he sounded out the possibility of replacing him with Scullin, who in 1930 had arranged the appointment of Sir Isaac Isaacs as the first Australian-born Governor-General. Then, in November 1943, he acceded to a suggestion from London to appoint not an Australian but King George VI's brother, the Duke of Gloucester. Curtin had to accept some caucus criticism of the decision, but it had the desired effect of emphasising loyalty to Britain, loyalty that had sustained some damage after his December 1941 'call to America', the controversies around the defence of Singapore, and his close relationship with MacArthur. Curtin may also have hoped that Gloucester's presence might help to make a British base in Australia more likely in a Pacific War that some thought would continue for many more years.[355] Now developing in Curtin's mind was the idea of a 'Fourth Empire', or the restoration of British power in Australia's region, "less to help in the defeat of Japan than to help secure the region when the war ended".[356]

By the end of 1943, Curtin's ministers were chafing, rather unrealistically, at Australia's exclusion from the deliberations of the Great Powers. Australia had no part, for example, in the November 1943 Cairo Conference at which the leaders of the United States, Britain and China made decisions about post-war Asia. This led to the Curtin Government's (mainly Evatt's) formulation of the agreement for mutual collaboration in the Pacific between Australia and New Zealand in January 1944 (the ANZAC Agreement), a surprise to Churchill and Roosevelt and not a pleasant one.[357]

Curtin was not in good health when, accompanied by Elsie part of the way, he visited the United States, Canada and Britain from April to June 1944. Meetings with Roosevelt and the US Secretary of State, Cordell Hull, did not go well as the Americans were irritated by some of Evatt's pronouncements on the ANZAC Agreement. Dogged by continuing poor health in England, Curtin nonetheless sought to mend the relationship with Churchill and to press ideas for improved co-ordination of imperial foreign policy by proposing a Secretariat for the (British) Commonwealth, twenty years before one was established.[358] In doing so, he pursued limited, even old-fashioned, foreign policy ideas, when contrasted with the forward-looking liberal internationalist approach taken by Evatt and Chifley after Curtin's death.[359] But Curtin's greatest international contribution was in acceding in 1942 to the Anglo-American Mutual Aid Agreement, which was concerned, among other things, with provision of reciprocal 'lend-lease' assistance between Australia and the United States. Under this agreement, Australia was committed to post-war international collaboration to reduce barriers to international trade. In the long term this committed Australia to move away from dependence on preferential trade with Britain to the more open trading system that would be buttressed by the International Monetary Fund and the General Agreement on Tariffs and Trade.[360]

On his return to Australia, Curtin was not the same man. As his health declined, he became increasingly irritable and less willing to tolerate criticism. Early in November 1944 he suffered a heart attack and was confined to hospital in Melbourne for two months. After returning to duty in January 1945 he was only capable of intermittent work. Late in April 1945 he had to return to hospital for treatment of congestion of the lung. Three months later, on 5 July 1945, he died peacefully at the Prime Minister's Lodge, aged a few days short of 60 and a half years. On the day of Curtin's death, Scullin, who had first-hand experience of the effect of stress on health of leaders, remarked that: "His end teaches us that it is not hard work, either mental or physical, that kills a man; it is anxiety and worry".[361] Curtin's death produced a sense of shock and grief among all Australians who had now witnessed the defeat of Germany but not yet Japan's.[362] Menzies, who had replaced Hughes as Leader of the UAP, spoke now not of a political adversary but of a martyr to the nation in war: "Nobody, whether political friend, or political foe, could dispute the single-mindedness, zeal, industry and devotion with which Mr. Curtin attacked his greatest task after becoming Prime Minister".[363]

After a state funeral in Canberra on 6 July, his body was flown to Perth, where on 8 July 100,000 people, one-third of the city's population, lined the six kilometre route to the Presbyterian section of Karrakatta cemetery beside which 25,000 people were attending his graveside.[364] Mourners extended from Elsie and other members of his close family, to the highest echelons of state: Frank Forde, the new Prime Minister, Menzies and Fadden, leaders of the respective opposition parties, Blamey and a host of state and federal politicians from all sides of politics. This was a state funeral but one with many humble touches that reflected the man; an accompanying film displayed interesting facts about Curtin from the "simplicity of his home life to many of his achievements".[365] "Never", wrote the *Kalgoorlie Miner* of this first funeral broadcast to the eastern states, "had the people of the State been so stirred over the death of a public man".[366] The mourning for Curtin extended from Perth to the eastern states and beyond Australia's shores to Churchill, MacArthur and Eleanor Roosevelt, who had lost her own husband on 12 April. In the words of the Presbyterian Pastor, Curtin "had literally laid down his life for mankind".[367] Two days after his death, the poet Dame Mary Gilmore published a poem:

JOHN CURTIN

What though we sent him forth
   With pomp and proud device,
Met for his epitaph
   Three words suffice:
'He saved Australia'.[368]

Legacy and Achievement

Rankings of Australia's prime ministers often give Curtin the highest place.[369] Major biographies by Ross, Day and Edwards all speak of his greatness and Edwards is in no doubt that Curtin remains Australia's greatest prime minister "in steadying the nation at a time of peril, but also in determining the shape of Australia's politics and economy for the following half century".[370] Yet Curtin did not have even four years as prime minister, while Menzies, accrued a total of eighteen years in that office. The most persuasive critique of Curtin, while not denying his accomplishments, concluded that:

> His isolationism has too often been called statesmanship by simple-minded patriots. He yielded responsibility over where Australia fought to his generals. Even in command of the home front, where he operated more effectively, he was at odds with the people he had to lead and had to be saved by his cabinet from turning austerity into tyranny.[371]

Any assessment of Curtin's political achievements must range beyond the prime ministership to include the significance of his leadership of the opposition from 1935 to 1941 and the feat of uniting and rebuilding the Labor Party after its catastrophic defeats in 1931 and 1934. Curtin was able to reconcile with the 'Langites' in 1936, putting Labor in a more competitive position for the 1937 election. Labor then almost wrested power from the coalition parties in 1940. Positioning Labor to recover from serious defeats and years in opposition was an accomplishment he shared with later Labor Prime Minister, Gough Whitlam.

A comparable achievement was his deft leadership of the opposition in the hung parliament after September 1940. Curtin offered constructive support to Menzies's wartime government and restrained impetuous colleagues pressing impatiently for power. He waited until the collapse of the Menzies and Fadden governments and, when he took power in October 1941, it was with legitimacy and support. This was a surprising achievement given the intractable internal divisions that he had to navigate and the difficult colleagues with whom he had to work. Curtin's idea of an Advisory War Council proved to be a successful instrument for the management of the House of Representatives in circumstances of minority government from 1940 to 1943; it also prepared senior Labor figures for ministerial office. His decision to reject Menzies's offer to join a national government was well-judged; it would certainly have unsettled Labor and possibly provoked a split and destroyed his leadership. Edwards and Souter both agree in portraying Curtin as a deceptively cunning player in the chess game of politics.[372]

The views of historians are divided over whether Curtin 'saved' Australia in 1942.[373] He proved to be prescient in calling for stronger air defences and criticising the degree of Australia's commitment in the United Kingdom and the Middle East from 1939 to 1941. Some historians, however, have argued that Japan did not have the intention or capacity to invade Australia in 1942 as Curtin and many others feared. What, they ask, was Curtin saving Australia from? Early in 1942, however, Curtin could not have known that Japan had decided not to invade Australia, and an invasion was not the only way that Australia could have been wrecked as either an economic or military power. Nor could he have been assured that the great naval encounters in the Coral Sea and Midway would necessarily be in America's favour.[374] Had they been in Japan's favour, Australia could well have been subject to naval blockade and raids on its northern coastline. In these circumstances, his insistence on the return of the AIF Divisions, in the face of objections of Churchill and Roosevelt, represents an extraordinary act of courage and fortitude. Curtin saw no alternative but to forge the close and dependent relationship with MacArthur that developed between 1942 and 1945, even if it meant loss of sovereignty that occasionally proved detrimental to Australia's national interests.

On the home front, Curtin's claims to greatness include his leadership for nearly two years of a minority Labor ministry that was able to govern in extraordinary circumstances with combination of competent administration, occasional compromises with the Opposition and superb management of the media. Curtin's increasingly national war leadership and successful mobilisation of Australia in 'total war' then helped Labor to achieve what was its most emphatic national political victory in 1943. The scale of Curtin's triumph meant that Labor was strongly placed as the nation moved from war to post-war reconstruction. It would oversee return to peacetime conditions in which many of the foundations of modern Australia were laid. The Curtin and Chifley Labor governments were able to rebuild Australia according to the political goals for which Curtin had striven all his life.[375] These included national control of the economy and of banking if not necessarily nationalisation. Major policy objectives were full employment and adequate provision of social services. The success of Robert Menzies's second period as prime minister from 1949 to 1966 was partly based on pragmatic and skilled management of the political settlement inherited from Curtin and Chifley. Australia emerged under Curtin's leadership a more independent and fully sovereign state. Another contribution was in not pressing in 1942 for a constitutional referendum for sweeping new national powers. This meant that the Australian federal system of government remained intact but of a different character. For the Commonwealth, now with uniform taxation, would be financially dominant.

Was Curtin Australia's greatest prime minister? Rankings of prime ministers, it must be admitted, are a questionable guide to the worthiness of major political figures and especially those at the apex. Prime ministers must be appraised in the circumstances in which they find themselves, the demands made upon them, the skills they bring to bear and the personal and character tests they face. For few of Australia's prime ministers has the road been so long and hard, the support so unsteady and uncertain, especially among their own ranks, as it was for John Curtin. It is easy in hindsight to quibble about Curtin's performance from winning the Labor leadership in 1935 to his death in 1945. The great mark of his achievement is that Labor was ready for national office when its opponents were revealed as catastrophically wanting; he steered the country through an existential crisis with purpose and assurance; and, when he died and a new era was in sight, Labor was in good order to shoulder the new burdens.

Endnotes

1. Don Whitington, *The House Will Divide: A Review of Australian Federal Politics*, Landsdowne Press, Melbourne, 1969, p. 57.
2. David Day, *John Curtin: A Life*, HarperCollins, Sydney, 1999, Chapter 1; John Edwards, *John Curtin's War Volume 1*, Viking/Penguin/Random House Australia, Sydney, 2017, pp. 15-18.
3. Lloyd Ross, *John Curtin: A Biography*, Macmillan, Melbourne, 1977, Chapter 1.
4. Ibid., pp. 6-7.
5. "John Curtin (1885-1945)", in John Ritchie, (ed), *Australian Dictionary of Biography, Volume 13*, Melbourne University Press, Carlton, 1993, p. 550.
6. Ross, *Curtin*, p. 10; Toby Davidson, *Good for the Soul: John Curtin's Life With Poetry*, University of Western Australia Press, Nedlands, 2021, p. 2.
7. Davidson, *Good for the Soul*, p. 199.
8. "Curtin Meets Mentor", *The Sun* (Sydney), 8 October 1937; Edwards, *John Curtin's War Volume 1*, pp. 16-17.
9. Peter Love, "Frank Anstey, Money Power and the Labor Split in War Time", *Victorian Historical Journal*, Vol. 86, No. 1, 2015, pp. 161-85.
10. See Nick Dyrenfurth and Frank Bongiorno, *A Little History of the Labor Party*, University of New South Wales Press, Sydney, 2011.
11. Paul Strangio and Nick Dyrenfurth, *Confusion: The Making of the Australian Two-Party System*, Melbourne University Press, Carlton, 2009.
12. John Nethercote, (ed), *Liberalism and the Australian Federation*, Federation Press, Annandale, 2001, pp. 93-6.
13. Ibid.
14. "Francis George Anstey (1865-1940)", in Bede Nairn and Geoffrey Serle, (eds), *Australian Dictionary of Biography, Volume 7*, Melbourne University Press, Carlton, 1979, pp. 79-81.
15. Day, *Curtin*, pp. 71-2.
16. "Ten Years Ago. Recollections and Reflections by Jack Curtin", *Socialist*, 27 August 1915.
17. "Thomas Mann (1865-1941)", Bede Nairn and Geoffrey Serle, (eds), *Australian Dictionary of Biography* (ADB), *Volume 10*, Melbourne University Press, Carlton, 1986, pp. 395-6.
18. Ross, *Curtin*, pp 17-24.

19   Ibid.

20   Quoted in "John Curtin (1885-1945)", *ADB, Volume 13*, p. 550.

21   "Ten Years Ago: Recollections and Reflections by Jack Curtin", *Socialist*, 27 August 1915; Liam Byrne, *Becoming John Curtin and James Scullin: The Making of the Modern Labor Party*, Melbourne University Press, Carlton, 2020, pp. 44-52.

22   Davidson, *Good for the Soul*, p. 23.

23   Ross, *Curtin*, Chapter 3; Byrne, *Becoming John Curtin and James Scullin*, pp. 82-6.

24   "Mr. Curtin's Career", *The Worker*, 9 July 1945.

25   Ross, *Curtin*, pp. 42-3; Day, *Curtin*, pp. 182-4.

26   "The Balaclava Contest", *Labor Call*, 20 August 1914.

27   Ibid.

28   Ibid.

29   Ross, *Curtin*, p. 32.

30   See David Day, *Andrew Fisher*, HarperCollins, Sydney 2015 and Laurie Fitzhardinge, *The Little Digger, 1914-1952: William Morris Hughes, a Political Biography, Volume 2*, Angus & Robertson, Sydney, 1979.

31   For Curtin's struggle with alcohol see Day, *Curtin*, pp. 145, 183-84, 221-22, and 302-3.

32   Ross, *Curtin*, pp. 43, 46 and 47; Edwards, *John Curtin's War Volume 1*, p. 22.

33   Davidson, *Good for the Soul*, pp. 88-9.

34   See Ernest Scott, *Australia During the War: The Official History of Australia in the War of 1914-1918, Volume 11*, Angus & Robertson, Sydney, 1940, Chapters 9 and 11 and Robin Archer, Joy Damousi, Murray Goot and Sean Scalmer, *The Conscription Conflict and the Great War*, Monash University Publishing, Clayton, 2016.

35   Byrne, *Becoming John Curtin and James Scullin*, pp. 101-5.

36   "Senator Lynch and Mr. Curtin. Statement about Gaol", *Daily News* (Perth), 27 September 1917; Day, *Curtin*, p. 233.

37   "Mr. J. Curtin Released from Gaol", *Daily Herald* (Adelaide), 16 December 1916. For the Hughes Government's use of the law against anti-conscriptionists see Catherine Bond, *Law in War: Freedom and Restriction in Australia During the Great War*, NewSouth, Sydney, 2020.

38   "Mrs Curtin", *Westralian Worker*, 8 May 1936; Day, *Curtin*, pp. 146, 148-9 and 149-51; Edwards, *John Curtin's War. Volume 1*, pp. 21-2.

39   Mrs Curtin", *Westralian Worker*, 8 May 1936.

40. "John Curtin", *The Australian Women's Weekly*, 28 September 1940.
41. Ibid.
42. Byrne, *Becoming John Curtin and James Scullin*, pp. 129-30.
43. "Send off for Jack Curtin", *Socialist*, 16 February 1917.
44. Day, *Curtin*, pp. 242-3.
45. Ibid.
46. Ibid., p. 266.
47. Davidson, *Good for the Soul*, p. 95.
48. Edwards, *John Curtin's War. Volume 1*, pp. 27-8.
49. See John Connor, *Anzac and Empire: George Foster Pearce and the Foundations of Australian Defence*, Cambridge University Press, Port Melbourne, 2011.
50. Davidson, *Good for the Soul*, p. 153.
51. Ross, *Curtin*, pp. 70-6: Day, *Curtin*, pp. 260-6; Edwards, *John Curtin's War Volume 1*, p. 31.
52. "Alexander McCallum (1877-1937)", in Bede Nairn and Geoffrey Serle (eds), *Australian Dictionary of Biography, Volume 10*, Melbourne University Press, Carlton, 1986, pp. 209-11.
53. "Phillip Collier (1873-1948)" in Bede Nairn and Geoffrey Serle, (eds), *Australian Dictionary of Biography, Volume 8*, Melbourne University Press, Clayton, 1981, pp. 70-2.
54. Ibid., p. 70.
55. "Curtin Guilty of Improper Statement", *The Daily News* (Perth), 19 December 1917.
56. Ross, *Curtin*, Chapter 6.
57. Ibid., pp. 19, 77 and 114.
58. Ross, *Curtin*, p. 81; Stuart Macintyre, *The Reds: The Communist Party of Australia from Origins to Illegality*, Allen & Unwin, Sydney, 1999, pp. 18-19.
59. For example, "Sunday Night Meeting at the Socialist Hall. Speech by Mrs Walsh and Jack Curtin", *Socialist*, 26 April 1918; Martin Pugh, *The Pankhursts: The History of One Radical Family*, Vintage, London, 2008; Davidson, *Good for the Soul*, p. 99.
60. Day, *Curtin*, pp. 290-1; Peter Gifford, *No Winners: the British Seamen's Strike of 1925*, Hesperian Press, Victoria Park, 2005.
61. "Geneva Labour Conference. Mr. J. Curtin nominated", *The West Australian*, 16 April 1924.
62. "International Labor Conference. Mr. J. Curtin Comments", *The Australian Worker*, 3 September 1924; "Labour Conference. Mr.

Curtin's Complaints", *The Western Mail* (Perth), 10 July 1924; Day, *Curtin*, pp. 284-6; Edwards, *John Curtin's War. Volume 1*, p. 29.

63 "The Fremantle Election. Mr. John Curtin's Candidature", *The Advertiser* (Fremantle), 16 October 1925.

64 Ibid.

65 "William Watson (1864-1938)", in John Ritchie, (ed), *Australian Dictionary of Biography, Volume 12*, Melbourne University Press, Carlton, 1990, pp. 407-8.

66 "Fremantle Seat. Close Contest Expected", *The West Australian*, 31 October 1928; Day, *Curtin*, pp. 297-8.

67 "Sir Frank Ernest Gibson (1878-1965)", in Christopher Cunneen, (ed), *Australian Dictionary of Biography, Supplemental Volume*, Melbourne University Press, Carlton, 2005, pp. 140-1.

68 "Sir Henry Keith Watson (1900-1973)", in John Ritchie and Diane Langmore, (eds), *Australian Dictionary of Biography*, Volume 16, Melbourne University Press, Carlton, 2002, pp. 502-3.

69 Ibid.

70 "Letter to the editor" from John Curtin, *The Australian Worker*, 5 October 1927.

71 Ross, *Curtin*, pp. 85-7; "Florence Mildred Muscio (1882-1964)" in Bede Nairn and Geoffrey Serle, (eds), *Australian Dictionary of Biography. Volume 10*, Melbourne University Press, Carlton, 1986, p. 651.

72 See John Robertson, *J. H. Scullin: A Political Biography*, University of Western Australia Press, Nedlands, 1974.

73 The relationship is comprehensively examined in Byrne's, *Becoming John Curtin and James Scullin*.

74 Quoted in Davidson, *Good for the Soul*, p. 165.

75 "Labor Campaign", *The Advertiser* (Fremantle), 9 November 1928.

76 Day, *Curtin*, pp. 303-5.

77 "John Curtin", *The Australian Women's Weekly*, 28 September 1940; Davidson, *Good for the Soul*, p. 199.

78 Minutes of Federal Parliamentary Labor Party, Canberra, 5 February 1929 in Patrick Weller and Beverley Lloyd, (eds), *Caucus Minutes: 1901–1949, Volume 2*, Melbourne University Press, Melbourne, 1975, pp. 324-5.

79 "Fremantle Contest. Reply to Mr. Curtin", *The West Australian*, 2 September 1929.

80 "Arbitration – Federal Withdrawal", *The West Australian*, 29 June 1929.

81	Ibid.
82	Dagmar Carboch, *The Fall of the Bruce – Page Government*, F.W. Cheshire, Melbourne, 1958, pp. 119-74.
83	"Fremantle Contest. Reply to Mr. Curtin", *The West Australian*, 2 September 1929.
84	Ibid.
85	"Election Figures – Fremantle electorate 1929", http://john.curtin.edu.au/fremantle/stats/1929.html
86	David Lee, *Stanley Melbourne Bruce: Australian Internationalist*, Continuum (Bloomsbury), London and New York, 2010, pp. 90-2.
87	Ross Fitzgerald, *"Red Ted": The Life of E.G. Theodore*, University of Queensland Press, St Lucia, 1994.
88	"Caucus Chooses Labor Team", 23 October 1929.
89	Day, *Curtin*, pp. 308-9; Whitington, *The House Will Divide*, pp. 59-60; Warren Denning, *Caucus Crisis: the Rise and Fall of the Scullin Government*, Hale & Iremonger, Sydney, 1982, p. 52; Robertson, *J. H. Scullin*, pp. 178-9.
90	Frank Anstey, *The Kingdom of Shylock*, Labor Call Print, Melbourne, 1917.
91	See Boris Schedvin, *Australia and the Great Depression: A Study of Economic Development and Policy in the 1920s and 1930s*, Sydney University Press in Association with Oxford University Press, Sydney, 1970 and Alex Millmow, *The Power of Economic Ideas: The Origins of Macroeconomic Management in Australia, 1929–1939*, ANU E Press, Canberra, c.2010; Geoffrey Spenceley, *A Bad Smash: Australia in the Depression of the 1930s*, McPhee Gribble, Ringwood, 1990, pp. 29-39.
92	"Free Trade Unworkable", *The Daily News* (Perth), 17 July 1930.
93	See Peter Love, *Labour and the Money Power: Australian Labour Populism 1850–1950*, Melbourne University Press, Carlton, 1984, Chapters 5 and 6.
94	"Mr. Curtin's Visit. Will Asist Campaign", *The Daily News* (Perth), 28 March 1930.
95	Bernard Attard, "The Bank of England and the Origins of the Niemeyer Mission, 1921-1930", *Australian Economic History Review*, Vol. 31, No. 1, 1992, pp. 66-83.
96	Fitzgerald, *"Red Ted"*, pp. 291-2 and 294-5.
97	"The Financial Policy of the Commonwealth. Mr Curtin's Great Speech", *Westralian Worker*, 27 June 1930.

98	"Claude Albo de Bernales (1876-1963)" in Bede Nairn and Geoffrey Serle, (eds), *Australian Dictionary of Biography*, *Volume 8*, Melbourne University Press, Carlton, 1981, pp. 264-5.
99	"Mr. Curtin's View", *The West Australian*, 26 December 1930; "Gold Bonus. Mr. Curtin advocacy", *The West Australian*, 29 March 1930.
100	"Sir Robert Gibson (1863-1934)", in Bede Nairn and Geoffrey Serle (eds), *Australian Dictionary of Biography*, *Volume 8*, Melbourne University Press, Carlton, 1981, pp, 654-6.
101	See David E. Moore, *The Curse of Mungana*, Boolarong Press, Salisbury, 2017.
102	Frank Bongiorno, "Search for a Solution, 1923-1929" in Alison Bashford and Stuart Macintryre, (eds), *The Cambridge History of Australia Volume 2. The Commonwealth of Australia*, Cambridge University Press, Port Melbourne, 2013, p. 77.
103	Bede Nairn, *The "Big Fella": Jack Lang and the Australian Labor Party 1891-1949*, Melbourne University Press, Carlton, 1987; Frank Cain, *Jack Lang and the Great Depression*, Australian Scholarly Publishing, Melbourne, 2005.
104	Ross, *Curtin*, pp. 98-101; Day, *Curtin*, p. 321.
105	Davidson, *Good for the Soul*, p. 173.
106	"Elegant and Sagacious". 'Morning Herald' on John Curtin", *Westralian Worker*, 28 November 1930.
107	Davidson, *Good for the Soul*, p. 165.
108	"Francis George Anstey (1865-1940)", in Bede Nairn andGeoffrey Serle, (eds), *Australian Dictionary of Biography*, *Volume 7*, Melbourne University Press, Carlton, 1979, p. 80.
109	"Curtin Bitter", *Maitland Mercury*, 14 September 1931.
110	"Mr. Curtin Outspoken", *The Australian Worker* (Sydney), 17 June 1931.
111	Ibid.
112	"The 'Rehabilitation Plan': Mr. Curtin's Devastating Speech", *Westralian Worker*, 10 July 1931.
113	Ibid.
114	See Anne Henderson, *Joseph Lyons: The People's Prime Minister*, University of New South Wales Press, Sydney, 2011; Peter Hart, "Lyons: Labor Minister – Leader of the U.A.P.", *Labour History*, Vol. 17, 1969, pp. 37-51.
115	See Warren Denning, *Caucus Crisis* and Patrick Mullins, "Warren Denning and the Making of Caucus Crisis", *History Australia*, Vol. 18, No. 1, 2021, pp. 94-111.

116 Geoffrey Sawer, *Australian Federal Politics and Law, 1929-1949*, Melbourne University Press, Melbourne, 1963, pp. 42-3.

117 "Election Figures – Fremantle Electorate 1931", http://john.curtin.edu.au/fremantle/stats/1931.html

118 Denning, *Caucus Crisis*, p. 53.

119 Fitzgerald, "*Red Ted*", pp. 333-4. Curtin's reconciliation with Scullin took longer to occur.

120 Day, *Curtin*, pp. 327-30.

121 Ibid., pp. 330-4.

122 "Scullin or Curtin? Labor's Federal Leadership", *Sunday Times* (Perth), 18 February 1934; Ross, *Curtin*, pp. 141-2.

123 Ross, *Curtin*, pp. 141-2; Day, *Curtin*, pp. 336-7; Davidson, *Good for the Soul*, p. 183.

124 "The Fremantle Seat. Mr. Curtin's Candidature", *The West Australian*, 8 September 1934.

125 Ibid.

126 "Anti-Labor Nominee for Fremantle. Mr H. K. Watson May Be Mr Curtin's Opponent", *Daily News* (Perth), 17 August 1934.

127 "Mr. Curtin's Election Campaign", *Westralian Worker*, 14 September 1934.

128 Ibid.

129 "Fremantle. Mrs Cardell-Oliver's Strong Fight", *The West Australian*, 17 September 1934.

130 "Election Figures – Fremantle Electorate 1934", http://john.curtin.edu.au/fremantle/stats/1934/html. The Social Credit Party was an Australian political party based on the Social Credit theory of monetary reform first set out by the British engineer, Clifford Douglas. It gained its strongest result in Queensland in 1935.

131 "Mr. Curtin's Intentions", *The Argus*, 6 March 1936.

132 Sawer, *Australian Federal Politics and Law*, pp. 73-4; Edwards, *John Curtin's War, Volume 1*, pp. 61-2.

133 "Labor's New Leader", *Truth* (Brisbane), 6 October 1935.

134 Byrne, *Becoming John Curtin and James Scullin*, pp. 162-3; Edwards, *John Curtin's War, Volume 1*, pp. 60-2.

135 Ross, *Curtin*, pp. 150-1.

136 David Day, *Curtin*, pp. 396-7, has reports of Curtin continuing to drink alcohol into the 1930s.

137 "Federal Labor Leader Mr. Curtin Chosen", *Shepparton Advertiser*,

2 October 1935.

138 Day, *Curtin*, p. 341; Ross, *Curtin*, p. 148; Davidson, *Good for the Soul*, p. 183.

139 Ross, *Curtin*, p. 148.

140 Whitington, *The House Will Divide*, p. 61.

141 John Manning Ward, "The Dismissal", in Heather Radi and Peter Spearitt, (eds), *Jack Lang*, Hale & Iremonger, Sydney, 1977, pp. 160-78.

142 Stuart Macintyre, *The Oxford History of Australia. Volume 4, 1901–1942 The Succeeding Age*, Oxford University Press, Melbourne, 1986, pp. 273-4; Lee, *Stanley Melbourne Bruce*, pp. 98-100.

143 Ross, *Curtin*, pp. 150-54.

144 Ibid., pp. 154-5; Nairn, *The "Big Fella"*, pp. 276-8.

145 For Australia's policies and attitudes to 'appeasement' see Christopher Waters, *Australia and Appeasement: Imperial Foreign Policy and the Origins of World War II*, I.B. Tauris, London, 2012; and Eric Andrews, *Isolationism and Appeasement: Reactions to the European Crises, 1935–1939*, Canberra, 1970; and David Bird, *J.A. Lyons, the Tame Tasmanian: Appeasement and Rearmament in Australia*, Australian Scholarly Publishing, North Melbourne, 2008.

146 Day, *Curtin*, pp. 344-5.

147 Ibid., pp. 532-3.

148 Ian Hamill, *The Strategic Illusion: the Singapore Strategy and the Defence of Australia and New Zealand, 1941–1942*, Singapore University Press, Singapore, 1981.

149 "Henry Douglas Wynter (1886-1945)", in John Ritchie and Diane Langmore, (eds), *Australian Dictionary of Biography, Volume 16*, Melbourne University Press, Carlton, 2002, pp. 599-600; Day, *Curtin*, pp. 350-2.

150 "Mr. Curtin Defends Labor Policy", *Sydney Morning Herald*, 6 November 1936; Edwards, *John Curtin's War, Volume 1*, pp. 119-23.

151 "Mr. Curtin Defends Labor Policy", *Sydney Morning Herald*, 6 November 1936.

152 Ibid.

153 "If Labor Wins Double Dissolution?", *Newcastle Morning Herald and Miners' Advocate*, 10 August 1937.

154 Nairn, *The "Big Fella"*, p. 290.

155 "Labour Election Policy. Mr. Curtin Announces at Fremantle", *Canberra Times*, 21 September 1937.

156 Ibid.

157 Ibid.
158 Edwards, *John Curtin's War, Volume 1*, p. 106.
159 Ibid.
160 "Labour Election Policy. Mr. Curtin Announces at Fremantle", *Canberra Times*, 21 September 1937.
161 Ibid.
162 "Government Returned with Reduced Majority", *Shepparton Adveriser*, 25 October 1937.
163 Geoffrey Sawer, *Australian Federal Politics and Law, 1929–1949*, pp. 99-100.
164 Whitington, *The House Will Divide*, p. 62.
165 Ibid., p. 58.
166 Ben Pimlott, *Hugh Dalton*, Macmillan, London, 1985.
167 Hugh Dalton typescript notes on Australia n.d. 1938, NLA: Dalton Papers, Australian Joint Copying Project M2612-2615, File 55. Dalton's view was echoed by the journalist Warren Denning, *Caucus Crisis*, p. 51. Denning remarked: "Although it is not easy to choose between Mr. Curtin, Mr. Scullin, and Mr. Anstey, Mr. Curtin is probably the finest speaker the national Parliament has produced since its transfer to Canberra".
168 Ibid.
169 David Faber, *Munich, 1938: Appeasement and World War II*, Simon & Schuster, New York, 2010.
170 Day, *Curtin*, pp. 360-3.
171 Ibid., pp. 369-70.
172 Edwards, *John Curtin's War, Volume 1*, p. 198.
173 See A.W. Martin, *Robert Menzies. A Life Volume 1 1894–1943*, Melbourne University Press, Carlton, 1993; Troy Bramston, *Robert Menzies: The Art of Politics*, Scribe, Brunswick, 2019.
174 Martin, *Menzies*, pp. 260-3.
175 "Mr. Curtin's Attack", *The Northern Herald* (Cairns), 15 March 1939.
176 Fitzhardinge, *The Little Digger*, p. 650.
177 See Stephen Wilks, *"Now is the Psychological Moment": Earle Page and the Imagining of Australia*, ANU Press, Canberra, 2020.
178 Martin, *Menzies*, pp. 269-67.
179 Ibid., pp. 274-5.
180 Alan J. Foster, "An Unequivocal Guarantee? Fleet Street and the British Guarantee to Poland, 31 March 1939", *Journal of*

Contemporary History, Vol. 26, No. 1, 1991, pp. 33-47.

181 Volker Ullrich, *Hitler: A Biography. Volume II. Downfall 1939-1945*, London, 2021, Chapter 2.

182 Quoted in Martin, *Menzies*, p. 284.

183 *Daily Telegraph*, 5 September 1939.

184 Day, *Curtin*, p. 373.

185 Minutes of the full Cabinet Meeting, Melbourne, 26 September 1939, National Archives of Australia (NAA), A2697/XR1, Vol. 2.

186 Martin, *Menzies*, pp. 289-91.

187 Ibid., pp. 291-3.

188 "Mr. Curtin Speaks for Labor", *The Evening News* (Rockhampton), 11 September 1939.

189 Day, *Curtin*, pp. 375-6.

190 See the varying views of historians see Martin, *Menzies*, p. 291; David Day, *The Great Betrayal: Britain, Australia and the Onset of the Pacific War, 1939–42*, Angus & Robertson, Sydney, 1988; and David Horner, *High Command: Australia and Allied Strategy, 1939–1945*, Allen & Unwin, Sydney, 1982, pp. 288-93.

191 Day, *Curtin*, pp. 278-9.

192 John Lukacs, *Five Days in London May 1940*, Yale University Press, New Haven, 1999.

193 Michael Korda, *Alone: Britain, Churchill and Dunkirk: Defeat into Victory*, WW Norton and Co., New York, 2017.

194 Philip Williamson, *National Crisis and the National Government. British Politics, the Economy and Empire, 1926-1932*, Cambridge University Press, Cambridge, 1992.

195 Nick Smart, *The National Government, 1931-1940*, Macmillan, London, 1999.

196 Kevin Jefferys, *The Churchill Coalition and Wartime Politics, 1940–1945*, Manchester University Press, Manchester, 1991; J.M. Lee, *The Churchill Coalition, 1940–1945*, Archon Books, Hamden Conn., 1980; and Leo McKinstry, *Attlee and Churchill: Allies in War and Peace*, Atlantic Books, London, 2019, Chapter 14.

197 Curtin, House of Representatives, 20 April 1939, John Curtin Prime Ministerial Library. Records of David Black. Abstracts of John Curtin's speeches in House of Representatives, Parliamentary Debates, 1938-1945, JCPML00784/6. Vol 159, 20 April 1939, pp. 19-21.

198 "Mr. Curtin's Prophecy", *Queensland Times* (Ipswich), 26 July 1940; Pat Weller, Bev Lloyd and Bron Stevens, "State Power and

Federal Intervention" in Radi and Spearitt, *Jack Lang*, pp. 224-6.

199 Nairn, *The "Big Fella"*, pp. 303-6
200 Day, *Curtin*, p. 379; Ross McMullin, *Light on the Hill: The Australian Labor Party 1891-1991*, Oxford University Press, Melbourne, 1991, pp. 201-2.
201 Nairn, *The "Big Fella"*, p. 305.
202 Letter from Curtin to Menzies, 20 June 1940, NLA: Menzies Papers, MS 4936, file 27.
203 Ibid.
204 Ibid., letter from Curtin to Menzies, 24 June 1940.
205 Ibid., letter from Menzies to Curtin, 12 July 1940.
206 Ibid.
207 Ibid.
208 "Election Speech of John Curtin delivered at Perth, 28 August 1940", https://electionspeeches.moadoph.gov.au/speeches/1940-john-curtin
209 Ibid.
210 Ibid.
211 Day, *Curtin*, p. 384. Hasluck, in *Government and the People, 1939–41*, p. 564, makes the same assessment.
212 Paul Hasluck, *Australia in the War of 1939-1945: The Government and he People, 1939-1941*, Australian War Memorial, Canberra, 1965, pp. 256-63; Sawer, *Australian Federal Politics and Law*, pp. 125-6.
213 "Mr. Curtin's Tour", *The Inverell Times* (New South Wales), 2 September 1940.
214 "Fremantle Seat. Keen Contest. Interview with Mr. F.R. Lee", *Fremantle Advocate*, 26 September 1940.
215 Day, *Curtin*, pp. 384-5; Davidson, *Good for the Soul*, p. 207.
216 "Curtin Wins", *The Daily News* (Perth), 28 September 1940.
217 "Election figures – Fremantle electorate 1940", http://john.curtin.edu.au/fremantle/stats/1940.html
218 Ross, *Curtin*, p. 197.
219 "Archie Galbraith Cameron (1895-1956)", in John Ritchie, (ed), *Australian Dictionary of Biography, Volume 13*, Melbourne University Press, Carlton, 1993, pp. 346-8.
220 Tracey M. Arklay, *Arthur Fadden: A Political Silhouette*, Australian Scholarly Publishing, North Melbourne, 2014; Arthur Fadden, *They Called Me Artie: the Memoirs of Arthur Fadden*, Jacaranda, Milton, 1969.

221 Letter from Menzies to Curtin, 30 September 1940, NLA: Menzies Papers, MS 4936 File 27.

222 Ibid., letter from Spender to Menzies, 3 October 1940.

223 "Advisory War Council Plan Accepted", *Mercury* (Hobart), 23 October 1940.

224 Hasluck, *Government and the People, 1939–1941*, pp. 270-1.

225 David Horner, *Defence Supremo: Sir Frederick Shedden and the Making of Australian Defence Policy*, Allen & Unwin, Sydney, 2000 and *Inside the War Cabinet: Directing Australia's War Effort, 1939-1945*, Allen & Unwin, Sydney, 1996.

226 Edwards, *John Curtin's War, Volume 1*, p. 149.

227 Ibid., p. 198.

228 Allan Martin and Patsy Hardy, (eds), *Dark and Hurrying Days: Menzies' 1941 Diary*, National Library of Australia, Canberra, 1993.

229 Martin, *Menzies*, p. 312.

230 "John Curtin (1885-1945)", *ADB, Volume 13*, p. 553; Martin, *Menzies*, p. 387.

231 "Evatt–Beasley as Dynamic Duo. Can Curtin Resist Them?", *Smith's Weekly* (Sydney), 17 May 1941.

232 Martin, *Menzies*, p. 308; Day, *Curtin*, pp. 403-4.

233 See Murphy, *Evatt*, Chapter 8.

234 Sawer, *Australian Federal Politics and Law*, p. 141.

235 Day, *Curtin*, p. 393.

236 Letter, Menzies to Casey, 8 December 1940, NLA: Menzies Papers, MS 4936, Consignment Received in 2000, file 30.

237 Ibid. This was Menzies's phrase and he referred to Evatt, Ward and Falstein.

238 Minutes of Advisory War Council Meetings, Canberra, 4 and 5 December 1941, National Archives of Australia (NAA): A5954, 812/1.

239 Minutes of the Advisory War Council, 5 February 1941, NAA: A5954, 812/1.

240 Ibid.

241 Ibid.

242 Ibid., Minutes of Advisory War Council, 11 February 1941.

243 Cablegram from Fadden to Menzies, 27 March 1941, NAA: A5954, 586/4.

244 Martin, *Menzies*, pp. 323-9; Jeffrey Grey, *A Military History of Australia*, Cambridge University Press, Cambridge, 1990, pp. 156-

7.

245 McKinstry, *Attlee and Churchill*, pp. 254-5.

246 Minutes of the Advisory War Council, 18 March 1941, NAA: A5954, 812/2.

247 *Gavin Long, Greece, Crete and Syria. Australia in the War of 1939-1945, Series 1 (Army). Volume 2*, Australian War Memorial, Canberra, 1953; Peter Ewer, *Forgotten Anzacs: The Campaign in Greece, 1941*, Scribe, Melbourne, 2016.

248 Martin, *Menzies*, pp. 348-9.

249 Ibid., p. 373-4.

250 Ibid., p. 379.

251 Minutes of the Advisory War Council, 14 August 1941, NAA: 5954, 813/1.

252 Letter from Curtin to Menzies, 26 August 1941, NLA: Menzies Papers MS 4936 Consignment Received in 2000, file 27.

253 Day, *Curtin*, p. 355.

254 Hasluck, The *Government and the People, 1939–41*, p. 564.

255 Whitington, *The House Will Divide*, pp. 78-82.

256 Letter from Frank Troy, Western Australian Agent-General in London to Curtin, 13 October 1941, NAA: A461, R4/1/12.

257 Ibid.

258 Ibid., letter from Curtin to Troy, 24 October 1941.

259 Clem Lloyd and Richard Hall, (eds), *Backroom Briefings: John Curtin's War*, National Library of Australia, Canberra, 1997 p. 15.

260 Whitington, *The House Will Divide*, p. 90.

261 *Digest of Decisions and Announcements*, No. 59, 6 June 1953 cited in David Black, *In His Own Words: John Curtin's Speeches and Writings*, Paradigm Books Bentley, 1995, p. 221.

262 Edwards, *John Curtin's War. Volume II. Triumph and Decline*, Viking, Melbourne, 2015, p. 17 and Day, *Curtin*, p. 433.

263 Ross, *Curtin*, p. 222.

264 Quoted in ibid., p. 223.

265 Gavin Souter, *Acts of Parliament: A Narrative History of the Senate and House of Representatives Commonwealth of Australia*, Melbourne University Press, Carlton, 1988, p. 350.

266 David Day, *Chifley: A Life*, Harper Perennial, Pymble, 2007.

267 John Nethercote, "The Office of the Leader of the Opposition in the House of Representatives", Master of Arts Thesis, Australian National University, November 1973, p. 83.

268 LF Crisp, *Ben Chifley: A Biography*, Longmans, Melbourne, 1963, p. 216.

269 Ross, *Curtin*, p. 224; Edwards, *Triumph and Decline*, p. 59; Paul Hasluck, *Diplomatic Witness: Australian Foreign Affairs, 1941-47*, Melbourne University Press, Carlton, 1980, p. 126.

270 Gideon Haig, *The Brilliant Boy: Doc Evatt and the Great Australian Dissent*, Simon & Schuster, Cammeray, 2021; John Murphy, *Evatt: A Life*, NewSouth, Sydney, 2016; Ken Buckley, Wayne Reynolds and Barbara Dale, *Doc Evatt: Patriot, Internationalist, Fighter and Scholar*, Longman Cheshire, Melbourne, 1994.

271 Whitington, *The House Will Divide*, p. 92.

272 Elwyn Spratt, *Eddie Ward: The Firebrand of East Sydney*, Rigby, Adelaide 1965; Paul Burns, *The Brisbane Line Controversy: Political Opportunism versus National Security*, Allen & Unwin, Sydney, 1998; Sue Rosen, *Scorched Earth: Australia's Secret Plan for Total War under Japanese Invasion in World War* II, Allen & Unwin, North Sydney, 2017.

273 Andrew Spaull, *John Dedman: A Most Unexpected Labor Man*, Hyland House, Melbourne, 1998.

274 Geoffrey Blainey, *The Steel Master: A Life of Essington Lewis*, Sun Books, Melbourne, 1981.

275 Samuel Furphy, (ed), *The Seven Dwarfs and the Age of the Mandarins: Australian Government in the Post-War Reconstruction Era*, ANU Press, Canberra, 2015.

276 Horner, *Defence Supremo*, pp. 158-9; Edwards, *John Curtin's War Volume 1*, pp. 285, 296.

277 See McKinstry, *Attlee and Churchill*, Chapter 19.

278 Caryn Coatney, *John Curtin: How he Won Over the Media*, Australian Scholarly Publishing, North Melbourne, 2016; Paul Strangio, Paul 't Hart and James Walter, *Settling the Office: The Australian Prime Ministership from Federation to Reconstruction*, Miegunyah Press, Carlton, 2016, pp. 207-8 and 215-16.

279 Davidson, *Good for the Soul*, p. 222.

280 Ibid.

281 Graham Freudenberg, *Churchill and Australia*, Macmillan, Sydney, 2008, pp. 313-14.

282 John Curtin, "The Task Ahead", 27 December 1941, http://john.curtin.edu.au/pmportal/text/00468.html

283 Cablegram from Curtin to Bruce, 3 December 1941, W. J. Hudson and H. J. W. Stokes, (eds), *Documents on Australian Foreign Policy. Volume V: July 1941-June 1942*, Australian Government Publishing

Service, Canberra, 1982 p. 267.

284 Ibid., cablegram from Curtin to Churchill, 23 January 1942, pp. 463-4.

285 Brian Farrell, *The Defence and Fall of Singapore 1940-1942*, Tempus, Stroud, 2005; Janet Uhr, *Against the Sun: The AIF in Malaya, 1941-42*, Allen & Unwin, St Leonards, 1998.

286 *Sydney Morning Herald*, 17 February 1942.

287 *Sydney Morning Herald*, 20 February 1942.

288 Bob Wurth, *Saving Australia: Curtin's Secret Peace with Japan*, Lothian Books, South Melbourne, 2006 and *1942: Australia's Greatest Peril*, Pan Macmillan, Sydney 2010.

289 Peter Stanley, *Invading Australia: Japan and the Battle for Australia*, Penguin Australia, Camberwell, 2008; David Horner, *Crisis of Command: Australian Generalship and the Japanese Threat 1941–1943*, Australian National University Press, Canberra, 1978. See also Henry P. Frei, *Japan's Southward Advance and Australia: from the Sixteenth Century to World War II*, University of Hawaii Press, Honolulu, c. 1991.

290 Fitzgerald, *"Red Ted"*, pp. 393-401.

291 David Lee, "Politics and government", in Joan Beaumont, (ed), *Australia's War, 1939–1945*, Allen & Unwin, Sydney, 1996, p. 94.

292 Paul Hasluck, *The Government and the People, 1942–1945*, Australian War Memorial Canberra, 1970. p. 633.

293 Freudenberg, *Churchill and Australia*, Chapter 23.

294 Edwards, *Triumph and Decline*, Chapter 1.

295 Day, *Curtin*, p. 457; Caryn Coatney, "Curtin: A Fighter for the Underdog", Museum of Australian Democracy, 2016, https://primeministers.moadoph.gov.au/collections/curtin-a-figher-for-the-underdog

296 Edwards, *Triumph and Decline*, Chapter 2.

297 General Douglas MacArthur, *Reminiscences*, McGraw-Hill, New York. 1964, p. 151.

298 Cablegram from Evatt to Curtin, 7 May 1942, NAA: A5954, 569/1.

299 Cablegram from Casey to Curtin, 15 March 1942, *DAFP, Volume V*, pp 640-2.

300 Ibid., cablegram from Curtin to Casey, 17 March 1942, p. 643.

301 Edwards, *Triumph and Decline*, pp. 26-30 and Day, *Curtin*, p. 461-5; Ross, *Curtin*, pp. 271-5.

302 Gavin Long, *The Six Years War: Australia in the 1939-1945 War*, The Australian War Memorial and the Australian Government

Publishing Service, Canberra, 1973, p. 181.

303 Ibid., p. 258; Peter Edwards, "Curtin, MacArthur and the 'surrender of sovereignty', a historiographical assessment", *Australian Journal of International Affairs*, Vol. 55, No. 2, 2001, p. 177.

304 Henry Stimson, US Secretary of War, citing MacArthur and quoted in Christopher Thorne, *Allies of a Kind: The United States, Britain and the War Against Japan, 1941-1945*, Oxford University Press, Oxford, 1978, p. 263.

305 Russell Parkin and David Lee, *Great White Fleet to Coral Sea: Naval Strategy and the Development of Australia–United States Relations*, Department of Foreign Affairs and Trade, Canberra, 2008, Chapter 5.

306 Hasluck, *The Government and the People, 1942-1945*, p. 349.

307 Peter Love, "Curtin, MacArthur and Conscription, 1942-43", *Historical Studies*, Vol. 17, No. 69, 1977, p. 505.

308 Quoted in John Curtin (1885-1945)', *ADB, Volume 13*, p. 556.

309 Curtin Press briefing 20 November 1942 in Lloyd and Hall (eds), *Backroom Briefings*, pp. 105-6.

310 Ibid., p. 106.

311 Spratt, *Eddie Ward*, p. 83.

312 Edwards, *Triumph and Decline*, pp. 143-61.

313 Stuart Macintyre, *Australia's Boldest Experiment*: War and Reconstruction in the 1940s, NewSouth Publishing, Sydney, 2015, pp. 134-7; Hasluck, *Government and the People 1942-1945*, pp. 326-53.

314 See Rodney Maddock, "Unification of Income Taxes in Australia", *Australian Journal of Politics and History*, Vol. 28, No. 3, 1982, pp. 354-66.

315 Gregory McMinn, *Nationalism and Federalism in Australia*, Oxford University Press, Melbourne, p. 264.

316 Brian Galligan, *Politics of the High Court: A Study of the Judicial Branch of Government in Australia*, University of Queensland Press, St Lucia, 1987, pp. 130-1. See also Souter, *Acts of Parliament*, pp. 350-1.

317 *Sydney Morning Herald*, 24 July 1942.

318 Hasluck, *Government and the People, 1942-45*, p. 321.

319 David Lee, "States' Rights and Australia's Adoption of the Statute of Westminster, 1931–1942", *History Australia*, Vol. 13, No. 2, 2016, pp. 258-74.

320 Hasluck, *Government and the People, 1942-45*, p. 12; Kosmas Tsokhas, "Dedominionisation: the Anglo-Australian Experience, 1939–

1945", *Historical Journal*, Vol. 37, No. 4, 1994, pp. 861-83.

321 Hasluck, *Government and the People, 1942–45*, p. 297. See also Horner, *High Command*, pp. 263-4.

322 Sydney Butlin and Boris Schedvin, *War Economy, 1942-1945*, Australian War Memorial, Canberra, p. 382.

323 Horner, *High Command*, p. 267.

324 Peter Edwards, "Curtin, MacArthur and the 'surrender of sovereignty'", p. 182. See also David Day, *Reluctant Nation: Australia and the Allied Defeat of Japan, 1942-45*, Oxford University Press, Melbourne, 1992, pp. 160, 172 and 190.

325 Parkin and Lee. *Great White Fleet to Coral Sea*, p. 171-2

326 Martin, *Menzies*, pp. 406-7, 408-10, and 416-17.

327 Quoted in Day, *Curtin*, p. 503.

328 See Burns, *The Brisbane Line Controversy*; Day, Curtin, 503-5; and Edwards, *Triumph and Decline*, Chapter 10.

329 According to the Journalist, Edgar Holt, Curtin had "won the debate hands down", *Sydney Morning Herald*, 23 June 1943; Souter, *Acts of Parliament*, pp. 356-7.

330 *Commonwealth Parliamentary Debates*, House of Representatives Vol. 175, 24 June 1943, p. 353.

331 Edwards, *Triumph and Decline*, p. 228.

332 "Federal Election Speech of John Curtin", Perth, 26 July 1943, https://electionspeeches.moadoph.gov.au/speeches/1943-john-curtin

333 Ibid.

334 Day, *Curtin*, p. 510.

335 *Sydney Morning Herald*, 19 August 1943.

336 Martin, *Menzies*. p. 412.

337 Hal Colebatch, *Australia's Secret War: How Unions Sabotaged Our Troops in World War II*, Quadrant Books, Sydney, 2013.

338 Hasluck, *Government and the People, 1942–45*, pp. 248-63 and 388-96.

339 Martin, *Menzies*, pp. 408-12; Hasluck, *Government and the People, 1942-1945*, pp. 365–71.

340 Ibid., p. 416.

341 Sawer, *Australian Federal Politics and Law*, pp. 157-8

342 Hasluck, *The Government and the People, 1942-45*, pp. 365-70.

343 Sawer, *Australian Federal Politics and Law*, p. 140.

344 W. J. Waters, "The Opposition and the 'Powers Referendum', 1944", *Politics*, Vol. 4, No. 1, 1969, pp. 42-56.

345 A.L. May, *The Battle for the Banks*, Sydney University Press, Sydney 1968; Warwick Eather and Drew Cottle, *Fighting from the Shadows: the Private Trading Banks, Political Campaigns and Bank Nationalisation* Australian Centre for Labour and Capital Studies, Shanghai, 2012.

346 Day, *Curtin*, p. 550.

347 Souter, *Acts of Parliament*, p. 362.

348 Lyndhurst Giblin, *The Growth of a Central Bank: The Development of the Commonwealth Bank of Australia* Melbourne University Press, Melbourne, 1951, chapters 8 and 12; Butlin and Schedvin, *War Economy, 1942-1945*, pp. 612-24.

349 Herbert Coombs, *Trial Balance*, Macmillan, South Melbourne, 1981, pp. 48-55.

350 L. F. Crisp, *Australian National Government*, Longman, Melbourne, 1970, pp. 447–8.

351 Ibid.

352 See Furphy, (ed), *The Seven Dwarfs and the Age of the Mandarins*.

353 See Hannah Forsythe, *A History of the Modern Australian University*, NewSouth Publishing, Sydney, 2014.

354 Day, *Curtin*, pp. 548-9.

355 Ibid., 524-5.

356 Edwards, *Triumph and Decline*, p. 245. See also James Curran, *Curtin's Empire*, Cambridge University Press, Melbourne, 2011.

357 See Robin Kay, (ed), *The Australian–New Zealand Agreement 1944*, Historical Publications Branch, Department of Internal Affairs, Wellington, 1972; Honae Cuffe, *The Genesis of a Policy: Defining and Defending Australia's National Interest in the Asia-Pacific, 1921-1957*, ANU Press, Canberra, 2021, Chapter 5; Hasluck, *Diplomatic Witness*, pp. 111-17.

358 Hasluck, *Diplomatic Witness*, pp. 136-9.

359 For Chifley's contribution to Australian foreign policy see Julie Suares, *J.B. Chifley: An Ardent Internationalist*, Melbourne University Press, Carlton, 2019.

360 John Edwards, *John Curtin's Gift: Reinterpreting Australia's Greatest Prime Minister*, Allen & Unwin, Sydney, 2005; and Roger Bell, *Unequal Allies: Australian-American Relations and the Pacific War*, Melbourne University Press, Carlton, 1977.

361 Robertson, *Scullin*, p. 472.

362 "Mr. Curtin's Death a National Loss", *Barrier Miner* (Broken Hill), 5 July 1945.
363 "Death of John Curtin. Great Wartime Premier", *The Evening Advocate* (Innisfail), 5 July 1945.
364 "Laid to Rest. Mr. Curtin's Funeral", *Kalgoorlie Miner*, 9 July 1945.
365 "The Late John Curtin. Funeral Film in Hands of the States", *Kalgoorlie Miner*, 19 October 1945.
366 "Laid to Rest. Mr. Curtin's Funeral", *Kalgoorlie Miner*, 9 July 1945.
367 Ibid.
368 Toby Davidson, *Good for the Soul*, p. 329.
369 For example, Paul Strangio, "Who Were Australia's Best Prime Ministers? We Asked the Experts", *The Conversation*, 21 August 2016 and Strangio, 't Hart and Walter, *Settling the Office*, p. 202.
370 Edwards, *Curtin's Gift*, p.157.
371 John Hirst, "Was Curtin the Best Prime Minister?", in *Looking for Australia: Historical Essays*, Black Inc, Melbourne, 2010, p. 197.
372 See Scuter, *Acts of Parliament*, p. 350.
373 A 1985 documentary film, "Hellfire Jack: the John Curtin Story" and a 2007 film for television, starring William McInnes as Curtin, made this argument.
374 Benjamin David Baker, "What if Japan Had Won the Battle of Midway?", *The Diplomat*, 8 January 2016.
375 In this argument Edwards's, *Curtin's Gift* is particularly persuasive.

Australian Biographical Monographs 16

www.ingramcontent.com/pod-product-compliance
Lightning Source LLC
Chambersburg PA
CBHW071453160426
43195CB00013B/2096